Gift MINDSET®

Unwrap the 12 Gifts to lead and live a life of purpose, connection and contribution

Renée Giarrusso

MACMILLAN

PRAISE FOR *GIFT MINDSET*

'*Gift Mindset* is a powerhouse of examples that can change culture in organisations and our everyday connection with the world. I highly recommend that all organisations use this book as a benchmark on how to drive a culture that inspires leadership.'

Michael Ritoli, General Manager, CUB Premium Beverages at Carlton & United Breweries

'*Gift Mindset* will help you build a human-centric culture, grow leadership and better understand people to get the best out of them to maximise performance. You will learn personal and professional strategies and gain the value of sharing and learning from mistakes and successes and how adopting a gift mindset makes anything possible. Renée has done it again, capturing wisdom from scholars, spiritual leaders, thought leaders and business leaders; however, it's the insight from her wealth of experience that shines through and is truly priceless. A wonderfully practical, educational, reflective and empowering read; certainly a 'go-to' resource.'

Karen Littlepage, Chief People & Culture Officer, GS1 Australia

'*Gift Mindset* is a must-read as a business and personal development tool. Renée has perfected the art of applying her own self-development stories and those of others to deliver easy to understand and remember methodologies for our own growth.

'The 12 Gifts are classic tools for any budding leader; I suggest you read and practise them often.'

Barry Borzillo, Managing Director and CEO, Intrax Consulting Group

'The key to living your best life – a life of purpose, connection and contribution – isn't circumstances, or pathology or talent. It's your mindset. In this book Renée unpacks the 12 specific gifts to focus on, including courage, resilience, gratitude and forgiveness.

‘Highly recommended for anyone who wants to have a more positive outlook on life but isn’t quite sure how to go about it.’

Peter Cook, Author of multiple books including *Implement*

‘A wonderful resource for our hearts and minds, beautifully written with personal experiences providing great examples of why these 12 Gifts matter and help us grow as human beings. Never before has such a book been more relevant and applicable in both our personal and professional lives. Self-reflection, self-awareness and acting on the ‘gift’ opportunities will enrich your life. After all, there is nothing for you to lose, and so much for you to gain. *Brava Renée!*’

Marie Varrasso, Head of Supply Chain, Officeworks

‘I have observed Renée working with our Metricon Regional teams, quickly identifying our key values and talent, then turning them into meaningful ways for us to better lead our teams for greater outputs.

‘The chapter on Resilience, in particular, resonated with me. Our teams continue to face increasing levels of pressure from both the office and customer environments. As a team we need to lean on our experiences and share our stories of recovery and strength just as Renée does here.’

Phil Barrett, General Manager, Regional Housing Victoria, Metricon Homes

‘As Renée shares her own family’s story of courage, a story familiar to many second and third generation Australians, she uncovers the key drivers of change and innovation. Her insights on how to build connectedness with our colleagues are particularly pertinent during a time when physical distance and flexible working practices are our new norm. *Gift Mindset* is a perceptive pathway towards deconstructing the things that unwittingly bind us and which we must unpack to forge forward with purpose.’

Joy Atacador, Partner and Australia Region lead of IP and Technology, Dentons

'Renée masterfully invites us into a place where we give ourselves permission to find, unwrap and enjoy gifts from all aspects of life and leadership. She reframes the challenges, contextualises the joys and makes sense of the everyday by handing us a framework to find and understand the gifts that can come from the work we do and the life we live.'

Rohan Dredge, Founder, New Level Leader; Co-Founder, For Leaders Global; Podcast Host and Author

'*Gift Mindset* is a guide and companion to help us navigate and learn from the daily challenges and opportunities we collide with through life. It's less about prescription and more about exploration of the situations, stories and happenings in our life. The 12 Gifts take us by the hand and lead us through the many ways to think and respond to what we experience. And the recipes... they're a bonus!

Lynne Cazaly, Award-winning Author, Keynote Speaker and Better Ways of Working Expert

'*Gift Mindset* is a fantastic read that all people can benefit from. Adopting the mindset to embrace our challenges, not just our successes, is a brilliant message on how we can build resilience and create optimism with those around us. I specifically enjoyed the message around being courageous by sharing our vulnerabilities. This is a leadership trait that I have tried to instil in myself throughout my career. It helps me to express myself while allowing me to connect at multiple levels across diverse cultures.

'I really enjoyed the read and would highly recommend it to others.'

Matthew Graham, Marketing Vice President, Mars Wrigley Confectionery Europe, Russia, CIS and Turkey

'I found this book full of really powerful lessons. It provides a roadmap full of tips and advice and practical ways to improve several areas of your life and business to overcome challenges and difficulties to live a life of purpose.

'The 12 Gifts are essential soft skills and by adopting the gift mindset you will live a fuller life, improve your emotional intelligence and positively impact workplace culture through more collaborative sharing.'

Ronan Leonard, Managing Director, Trnsform Asia Pacific

'Renée walks her talk with *Gift Mindset* and arms leaders, teams and organisations with practical strategies to create a self-leadership and sharing culture. This is the book every leader, team member, parent, student and child needs to create better workplaces for now and the future. I wish I had read this book years ago and I'll be passing it on to many of my own clients!'

Jane Anderson, Voted #3 Branding Expert Globally, Forbes Coaches Council, Certified Speaker, Award-Winning Writer, Coach and Author of seven books

'Renée, your entire book is a gift, in itself. A major take-away when diving into the Gift Timeline is that polar opposites will always bring you to a decision. Well done my friend, a great insight!'

Gilbert François, Managing Director, Earthlink Alliance

'*Gift Mindset* is a blueprint to discover beauty within our experience – from the chaotic and challenging to the pinnacles of joy, success and enlightenment. In this book, Renée offers a new path to individual, team and organisational growth and presence. Let it guide you to the hidden gems born of curiosity, vulnerability, courage and self-awareness.'

Stephen Scott Johnson, Change Leadership Expert and International Mentor; Author *Emergent – Ignite Purpose, Transform Culture, Make Change Stick*

'In this wonderful book, Renée explores what makes leaders, teams and individuals tick and she shares her gifts, passion and wisdom that will take your team from inertia to engagement.

'While Renée exudes all 12 mindsets, to me her greatest gifts are Resilience (shown from the day she interviewed at Mars), Connection (everyone loves working with Renée) and Reenergising (she sparks everyone with her unparalleled work ethic).

'Unwrap the 12 Gifts and be rewarded with leading drivers, barriers, tools, frameworks and your very own 'bomboniera'.'

Mark Truelson, Disruptor, Speaker, Mentor, Director UniBev-BDV, Innovation and Storytelling Expert

'Now more than ever we need connected and collaborative cultures and Renée's insights and messages in this book need to be taken on board by all organisations.

'I loved the practical tools that can be applied and shared in the workplace. This book is a treasure chest of resources, insights and stories we all need to bring into our lives.

Maria Palazzolo, Executive Director and Chief Executive Officer, GS1 Australia

'This book is like a beautiful painting, each brushstroke lovingly painted on the page, each gift unpacked slowly and deliberately, in a way that makes sense and makes me want to jump in and start improving myself immediately.'

Emma McQueen, Executive and Business Coach and Author of *Go-Getter*

'*Gift Mindset* is the gift that keeps giving! It is an incredible source of inspiration and reminds us to use our life experiences to shape our world, but not to define us.'

Dr Amy Silver, Speaker, Author, Facilitator

'A great book to immerse yourself in to find more meaning in your life and workplace. The reflections and practical examples are helpful, but what I really feel this book asks of us is to be curious as to how we can introduce change to gain greater meaning in our lives. I believe we already have the strength within us to do this, but sometimes we lose a bit of who we really are when we experience success or challenges. My favourite chapter was gratitude as it is a gentle practice we can all embrace to be kinder to ourselves.'

Angela Burr, General Manager Marketing and Commercial, Lactalis

'This is an essential guide for anyone who'd like to integrate past and current, challenges and success, in such a way that doesn't just provide more meaning and fulfilment in your life, but upgrades your ability to contribute back to the world.'

Maurice Schill, Founder and CEO, JuJu

'Renée is authentic, generous and shows strength in her vulnerability. The life lessons that consume many are crafted into gifts, which we can all appreciate and get enormous value from. Renée talks about deep self-awareness as a means for progress and she's captured this beautifully. *Gift Mindset* is a must-read for anyone wanting to thrive, not just survive!'

Kate Stewart, Founder and Managing Director, Stay tray

'I am grateful for the opportunity to co-create with Renée and help deliver the message of the times: "The world needs 'realistic and infectiously optimistic leaders' to be beacons of optimism in a fog of pessimism." The leader looks like the person in your mirror. In Chapter 7, Renée shares the Gift of Optimism that you can adopt to enhance your life and inspire those around you. I commend *Gift Mindset* to you.'

Victor Perton, CEO, Centre of Optimism

To my two amazing siblings,
Lyndelle and Dean,
who have taught me so much about
the Gifts of Resilience and Courage.
Both are living examples of
the power of the Gift Mindset.

First published in 2023 by Major Street Publishing Pty Ltd

First published in India 2023 by Macmillan
an imprint of Pan Macmillan Publishing India Private Limited
707 Kailash Building
26 K. G. Marg, New Delhi 110001
www.panmacmillan.co.in

Pan Macmillan, The Smithson, 6 Briset Street, Farringdon, London EC1M 5NR
Associated companies throughout the world
www.panmacmillan.com

ISBN 978-93-95624-89-3

1 3 5 7 9 8 6 4 2

Internal design by Production Works
Printed in India by Gopsons Papers Pvt. Ltd., Noida

CONTENTS

MEET RENÉE

Renée has been fascinated by people since childhood. She has always been drawn to those from other cultures and backgrounds, and has a curious mindset and love of learning. She is a connector, a collaborator and highly energetic and passionate about whatever she does. She started writing poetry and short stories from the age of eight, and knew within her heart she would one day be an author.

Renée is a highly sought after communication and leadership expert, leading teams and working with leaders for over 22 years. She is a keynote speaker, a professional educator, a mentor and a professional certified coach (PCC). She published her first book, *Limitless Leadership*, in 2016 and was a contributor to the *Leaders of Influence* anthology. She gains a great level of personal fulfilment from working with a range of clients to realise the transformational benefits that tailored development can provide at an individual and team level.

Throughout high school she had more than 11 part-time jobs. These included working in retail and hospitality, teaching dance, working at a modelling agency and, later, as a sales cadette for a newspaper and a brand manager for a coffee company. Renée ended up studying business and marketing and, following this, spent the next 15 years in senior sales, marketing and leadership roles in a large FMCG organisation. This experience taught her about leadership, adaptability and creativity, and fuelled her lifelong passion for learning and growing others.

Growing up, Renée wanted to be a performer, a nurse, a teacher and a journalist. It's uncanny that she now gets to enjoy combining of all these roles in the work she does with leaders and organisations as a speaker, educator, mentor and coach, and as an author.

Renée has always lived life to the fullest. Seeing people realise and achieve what is possible lights her up. She believes we are all limitless, and that the challenges we face and the successes we achieve make us who we are and who we are continually becoming. She passionately works with leaders, teams and organisations to accelerate leadership and communication to lift culture and performance.

Her 15 years' hands-on experience in senior leadership and sales roles gives her credibility and a deep understanding of what it takes to lead a high-performing collaborative team and develop positive and productive organisational culture. She is aware of the day-to-day workplace pressures and challenges to perform in today's corporate business environment. Those with whom Renée has worked appreciate her dynamic flair, energy, adaptability, wisdom and passion to assist others to grow and achieve even more success.

Renée is often on radio sharing her message and has had her inspirational insights and thought leadership published in *Huffington Post*, *Coaching Life*, *Retail World* and many more. She is the founder and host of the Limitless Leaders Podcast.

Renée's clients mirror the diversity of her experience and network. Some of the clients she has worked with include GS1 Australia, Metricon Homes, Intrax Consulting Engineers, Australia Post, Snack Brands Australia, JLL, George Weston Foods, World Vision, SPC, Master Builders, EY, ANZIIF, Pioneer Electronics, Cookers

Oil, Pall Corporation, Mazda, Openpay, Connecting2Australia, Harvey Norman, William Adams, Taylors Wines, Grain & Bake Co and many more.

In her spare time Renée loves to cook and entertain, travel, do yoga and continue her passion of learning and growing through and with others.

Connect with Renée

giftmindset.com

reneegiarrusso.com

linkedin.com/in/reneegiarrusso

facebook.com/ReneeGiarrussoConsulting

instagram.com/reneegiarrussoaustralia

@Renee_Giarrusso

PART I

THE GIFT MINDSET®

One

WHY THE GIFT MINDSET® MATTERS

> *I can be changed by what happens to me. But I refuse to be reduced by it.* —Maya Angelou

For many years I have embraced the Gift Mindset. As I shared the concept with others, they found that adopting this powerful mindset helped them to embrace challenges and successes, both in and out of the workplace. Sharing the lessons we learn through these gifts not only empowers us, but can be someone else's survival guide and can create a culture of sharing and openness.

In the first part of this book, you'll get a grasp of the concept of the Gift Mindset. Then, in part II, we explore the 12 Gifts. You can read these in any order, depending on your needs and what is important to you right now. A book has lived its purpose when it's dogeared, marked up and worn; my intention is that this book will become a go-to resource and a gift that keeps on giving.

But first, let me share with you my first gift.

My first gift

It was 1997 – the year *The Castle* movie was released and 'this is going straight to the pool room' become a much-loved Australian catchphrase. It was also the year Princess Diana tragically passed away and the *Titanic* became a worldwide hit on the big screen, with its theme song, 'My heart will go on', flooding our airwaves.

This was the year that I believe I first experienced what I call 'the Gift Mindset' – a year that changed me and my outlook on life forever.

I was in my early 20s; I had just completed tertiary study, come out of a relationship and was sick of studying. A switch flicked in me and I knew I wanted to travel and get outside my comfort zone. So, I decided to spend six months in Connecticut, USA, teaching dance at YMCA summer camps. Now that I reflect on it, this was quite an erratic thing to do, having never been overseas before. My poor mum nearly had a nervous breakdown and only now can I understand why.

This amazing experience included teaching 25 kids at any one time on two different camps; luckily for me, the popular Spanish dance song 'Macarena' had just come out – it was a great default dance to keep my under-six-year-old group occupied. I lived with host families, was bitten by a dog and hospitalised, and spent three months backpacking across the US on just US$2000.

I came back independent, worldly (so I thought) and energised as a person. The experience was challenging, but taught me so much about the world and myself. I guess the Gift of Growth was unwrapped in front of me during this time – I grew in every way possible.

On returning to Australia, I worked a few casual café jobs and utilised my marketing qualification within a small start-up coffee business, but I knew there was more for me. Serving croissants to corporate workers on their lunchbreaks and being locked in a small office next to the coffee roaster was not where I thought I would end up.

An opportunity

Before long a black-and-white newspaper advertisement for a job within a global company caught my eye. I ripped it out of the paper and pinned it on the cluttered corkboard in my bedroom. Maybe it was the visual – the advertisement didn't even have a job title. Instead, a slogan caught my eye. It said, 'Do you want Success?', and featured an M&M's character holding an upwards arrow. I jumped at the opportunity and got through five of six gruelling interview stages to apply for the role. It was down to me and one other candidate to present at a final assessment centre on a rainy Tuesday morning in July 1997. I slaved for hours creating a marketing presentation and rehearsing it. I had organised a lift into the city from a good friend, practised my presentation and even lashed out on yet another new outfit, all in the hope of securing the job.

I really wanted this job; it would be my first real professional job, where I would be paid what I believed I deserved. I could be the one ordering croissants in my lunchbreak at the café I had worked at. I would also get a car and be on my way to climbing the corporate ladder – both really important things to a 22 year old.

On the night before the presentation I received an unexpected phone call. I was out watching a movie when Mum called saying I needed to come home – something had happened. I will never forget that drive home with my now-husband, whom I had only just met. I was on autopilot. When we arrived at my mum and stepdad's house, where I was living at the time, Mum opened the door puffy-eyed and in tears. I was shocked to hear that my dad was in hospital. We got back in the car and sped to the hospital; in a blur of uncertainty and tears, we ran into emergency. My dad – whom I was very close to – had just passed away. I was overwhelmed.

Although he had just passed on, I got to hold his hand and say goodbye; he was only 51 years old.

It was the most surreal experience of my life. The nurse held me up as I was holding Dad's still-warm hand that had comforted me a million times, saying an emotional goodbye with little feeling of closure or comprehension of what had just happened.

Afterwards, we drove home to my family's house in numbed silence. We were all speechless from shock. We had so many questions, but nobody knew how to ask them.

Reality hits

Reality hit me when I remembered I had my job assessment the next morning. What was I going to do? Should I go? Should I cancel?

Dad and I were similar in many ways. He had been an avid entrepreneur in the rag trade and printing game with amazing ideas, dreams and a knack for technology and music; he would have loved to be alive in this day and age. Unusually, I hadn't seen him for over two weeks – the last thing he had said to me was, 'Get that job at Mars; it will set you up. I know you can get it.' With Dad's words in my mind, I called my friend Anna to let her know what had happened and to confirm that she could still drive me to the city.

With a foggy head and a heavy heart, I got ready the following morning, armed with my presentation and a stomach full of butterflies.

The assessment went well. I somehow put emotion aside and focused on getting the role. By the end of the process, I was emotionally and mentally drained, physically dizzy and only just hanging on. I'm not going to say it was easy; it was probably the most challenging thing I have ever done, but I had so much determination to win the role that nothing could stop me.

I ended up getting the job and spent over a decade with an amazing company. Some people may call me ruthless, insensitive and crazy – I even questioned myself at the time – but my optimism and positive outlook went into overdrive to get me through. This is an example of the motivation of optimism working for me. I knew that to move forward I needed to live life to the fullest, and I had to use this experience of losing my dad to drive me to live the life my father didn't get to live. This taught me the Gift of Resilience.

Challenges as well as successes

This experience taught me how much embracing our challenges, not just our successes, can teach us. Adopting a Gift Mindset is all about dialling up self-awareness and leaning into how you are feeling, then acknowledging and accepting the lesson the experience offers – as opposed to resisting it, struggling against it and letting it hinder you. Did I want my dad to open the door and look at me lovingly with his beautiful blue eyes and hug me and say it was all a bad dream? Yes of course I would have done anything for that to happen. I didn't choose or want this situation. I learnt to accept the reality and use resilience to drive me to make a difference in life, and embrace every day as if it were my last.

Energy and passion kicked in, like an electrical surge that took over my thoughts, my body and me as a person. This feeling has never left me – this is the foundation of the Gift Mindset.

Our biggest lessons come through embracing, not resisting, our challenges and successes. When we adopt a Gift Mindset we can approach situations in our lives with deeper self-awareness, viewing whatever we are faced with, good or bad, as an opportunity to progress. Seeing the gift in any situation changes our thoughts, feelings and therefore the way we approach our tests and triumphs.

Gifts can come in many forms. Sometimes they are hidden or buried in the past; sometimes they are sitting right under our noses;

other times an event we're in the midst of will become, at some point, a learning experience and a Gift.

Do you remember your first gift? It may not have been based on a challenge or tragedy, but a success. Maybe you won a sporting game or a scholarship, or maybe someone showed you empathy that got you through a hard time and now you use that gift with others. It's worth reflecting on what you have learnt and how you have applied this in your life and, in the process, shared it with others.

Losing my dad at such a pivotal time impacted how I approached my life, professionally and personally. On some days I broke down but, overall, I embraced what I could instead of resisting what I couldn't change. And now I want to share the Gift Mindset with you.

Are you ready to unwrap your gifts?

A Gift Mindset

Now that you have grasped the concept of having a Gift Mindset, you may be pondering two things:

1. Why does having a Gift Mindset matter?
2. What will it cost you, your team and your loved ones if you *don't* adopt this level of awareness and acceptance, applying what you have learnt from your gifts?

By adopting the Gift Mindset, we get to live our legacy now by living a life of purpose, connection and contribution.

Positive psychology research shows that 40% of our happiness is determined by how we think and act. It is possible to achieve an increase in our happiness – a key reason we need to adopt a Gift Mindset to move forward progressively and be happier and even more successful.

It is important to note that this mindset applies both in and out of a work context – as you read this, please ensure you wear both hats.

The 2020 global pandemic is an example of a situation presenting gifts that both challenge us and provide opportunities to look at success differently.

Why having a Gift Mindset matters

If we choose not to learn from and share our lessons, or close ourselves off from receiving lessons from others, we risk robbing the world of our insights or, worse, contributing mindlessly to a world already heavy with distraction and clutter.

Never before have we lived in a such connected world, but at the same time been so disconnected. Social media has been linked to elevated levels of loneliness, anxiety and depression, as well as decreased social skills.

In my experience, many people focus on broadcasting only the positive aspects of their lives. On most platforms, people are depicted as living their dream life – perfect relationships, endless holidays, picture-perfect plates of food and successful businesses. Social media has become a highlight reel of only the good; it rarely portrays what is truly going on. This can lead to 'comparison syndrome', where people compare their own 'real' lives with others' highlight reels – a natural human reaction. If you are comparing yourself to the digital presence of someone else, you run a high possibility of discounting yourself for reasons that aren't usually valid.

> *Comparison can be a killer; it can diminish and dim you as a person.*

Psychologist Leon Festinger developed social comparison theory in 1954, stating that individuals determine their own social and personal worth based on how they stack up against others around them. Subsequent research shows that people who compare themselves to others on a regular basis often experience feelings of guilt, dissatisfaction and sometimes even remorse.

Social media is a huge contributor to social comparison.

Don't compare your chapter 1 to someone else's chapter 20.

It is important to remember that no-one is you, and that is why sharing your gifts is vital. The sharing process can get you out of your own head, and reinforces your uniqueness. It gives you the ability to help others grow through your lessons, both positive and negative. Contribution is a core human need, as is connection: we are all wired to connect. By adopting a Gift Mindset, you satisfy these needs, not only for you but also for those around you.

Many of the successes and challenges shared via social media are topical, and often there is no evidence, no essence and no real connection to learn from. Don't get me wrong: I love technology and there is a use for it, but when it comes to sharing lessons, in many cases, these platforms are light on as far as what is real.

Social media is creating a paradox effect where we get the illusion of many choices when, in actual fact, we find it harder to find viable options. We may feel that by digitally connecting and sharing we are having social engagement, when essentially none of the connections are physical or real. I know I find this when shopping online; I often feel overwhelmed with choice, and end up buying nothing.

We all know that mobile phones, once a luxury and now an extension of most people's arms, have taken over. Recently at my local park I noticed seven dog walkers, each of them on their phones and not present in walking their furry friends. Research out of the UK indicates that one in eight of us is addicted to our phone, with an average of five to six hours spent on-screen daily.

Someone once said that the only two types of people who call their customers 'users' are drug dealers and app developers; I can see why!

People aren't having as many real, human-centred connections and interactions these days; the age of technology and distraction is upon us, and I can't see the landscape becoming any less cluttered.

In her book *Alone Together*, social psychologist Sherry Turkle argues that our relentless connection to the digital world is actually driving isolation. On the whole, she says, we are now 'lonelier and more distant from one another … the effect of this is that the way we interact online has changed and above all it has put a strain on our personal relationships, as well.'

Did you know that more than 65,000 Australians attempt suicide per year, with more than 3000 suicide deaths in 2018? Suicide has become the leading cause of death in Australia for people between 15 and 44 years of age, with reasons including stressful life events (imagine if we could share these openly), trauma, mental illness and substance abuse. In this age of distraction, we need to go back to human connection. I believe in my heart of hearts that the Gift Mindset could help us share more of ourselves, as a way of helping others.

Vulnerability and courage

The more open we are, the more vulnerable we become, and the more likely others will listen and use our lessons as a survival guide. Brené Brown's extensive research on vulnerability has bought to light its importance. We need to peel back the layers and understand our fears and feelings – these are connected to every success or challenge we experience.

Future leadership belongs to the brave and if this means sharing our lessons, we have a compelling reason to do so. Courage is a skill set we need to foster and master – as Brown says, 'The greatest barrier to courageous leadership is armour.'

The way we see and understand others in a real sense is dependent on trust, respect and what we are willing to share. Disclosing our challenges and our successes to others can help create rapport and support deeper and more meaningful relationships.

One day many years ago, back in my corporate life, my manager told me that he struggled with numbers. I was taken aback: how could he possibly struggle with what was such a large part of the role that he was so good at? As a sales director, his role was largely driven by budgets, scorekeeping and forecasting. He openly disclosed what he had done to upskill in this area, and how he had learnt to love numbers. This resonated with me – firstly because numbers have never been my strong point, either; but, more importantly, I was impressed that he had openly shared his weakness with me. I'll never forget that conversation and the Gift of Growth that he gave me. The lesson I took on board is to be open and honest and share what you need in order to be of service to others. I still can't say I love numbers, but I have learnt to like them. This lesson was a priceless reminder of how important it is to share ourselves with others.

When I reflect on people and situations, whether challenging or positive, it reinforces the importance of being aware of these experiences and knowing their drivers, which we will explore in the next chapter. The reasons to foster a Gift Mindset are strong and compelling, and the cost of not doing so means we leave the gifts under the Christmas tree, tightly wrapped, containing wasted gold. I ask you, 'Why waste what could be so priceless to ourselves and others?'

Two

THE FOUR DRIVERS OF A GIFT MINDSET®

The word '*gift*' simply means something given willingly to someone without payment; a present. As we know, gifts come in many forms. We can give gifts to others, receive gifts from others and we can give ourselves gifts such as self-compassion. In most cultures, gifts play an important role in developing healthy, loving relationships.

The term 'Gift Mindset' resonates with me. When we share our gifts by sharing our experiences and lessons, we strengthen our relationships with those around us.

Open, unwrap and use your gifts

Gifts come from experiences in both your personal and professional life. They could originate from:

- challenging situations or people
- positive situations or people.

Let's have a closer look at both types of gifts.

In 2016, the Japanese notion of *wabi-sabi* – meaning beauty that is imperfect, impermanent or incomplete, as opposed to our classical Western notion of beauty as perfect, enduring and monumental – made its way into homewares and industrial design. Many cafés and homes were built purposely leaving cracks in the walls, exposed beams and concrete floors, lopsided sugar jars on tables and earthy elements in their raw state scattered throughout. There were no perfect lines nor polished perfection to be seen anywhere – the rawness and imperfections were actually the focus, rather than being hidden away or covered up.

In Japan, an art form called *kintsugi* – the art of precious scars – involves using precious metals to repair broken ceramics. It gives a new lease on life to pottery that becomes even more refined thanks to its 'scars'. *Kintsugi* teaches us that broken objects are not something to hide, but to display with pride.

How similar are we as humans to *kintsugi* and *wabi-sabi*, with all of our scars, mistakes, lessons and the wisdom we learn in this thing called life? How often, as humans, do we hide the things that make us who we are today? I have always believed that where we are now, personally and professionally, is a result of our choices, lessons and mistakes along the way. Our scars make us stronger and more beautiful, and why not display these gifts in the same way *kintsugi* displays the art of precious scars?

Being human in today's world is more important than ever – we need to let our guards down, no matter who we are or what role we are in.

Your scars are someone else's signs of hope.

Volatility, uncertainty, complexity, ambiguity

The US military uses the acronym VUCA (volatility, uncertainty, complexity, ambiguity) to present the context in which organisations view their current and future states. This can also apply to you as an individual:

- Volatility refers to the nature and dynamics of change and the speed at which this occurs.
- Uncertainty relates to the lack of predictability and certainty of change – this is where our awareness and our understanding of issues and events is so crucial to our success.
- Complexity applies to the multiple forces, issues, chaos and confusion that can surround the organisations we are in.
- Ambiguity relates to the haziness of reality and the mixed meanings of everything we face.

To survive and thrive in such a fast-paced and challenging environment, we need to tap into the four areas of VUCA and adopt the Gift Mindset to share the lessons and wisdom of our mistakes, challenges and successes.

Mistakes and life's hard gifts and successes should never define you, but instead guide you through. Don't 'awfulise' and dwell on your challenges, but instead map out the lessons you have learnt and be a lighthouse for others who may benefit from what you've been through.

> *The scars you share become lighthouses for others who are headed for the same rocks as you hit.* —Jon Acuff

Many clients share with me the most amazing experiences and lessons they have learnt, but rarely do they share these with their teams or businesses. I challenge them on this and ask them to imagine what would be different for them if their manager had shared those same lessons with them earlier in their career. It's almost selfish not to share what you have learnt, providing you frame the lesson in a way that is useful and heartfelt, with good intention.

Over the last few years I've been sharing more of my story with clients and in keynotes, and the response has been positive. Knowing what to share and the intent is vital; don't share for the sake of being 'vulnerable'. Make sure you share your gifts with integrity and a rawness that encapsulates what happened, the result and the lesson that you learnt, good or bad.

The four drivers of a Gift Mindset

The four key drivers of the Gift Mindset include our challenges, our positive experiences, and the people and situations involved in these. These gifts can come in any combination and can be just as powerful and enriching to yourself as to those you may be sharing them with.

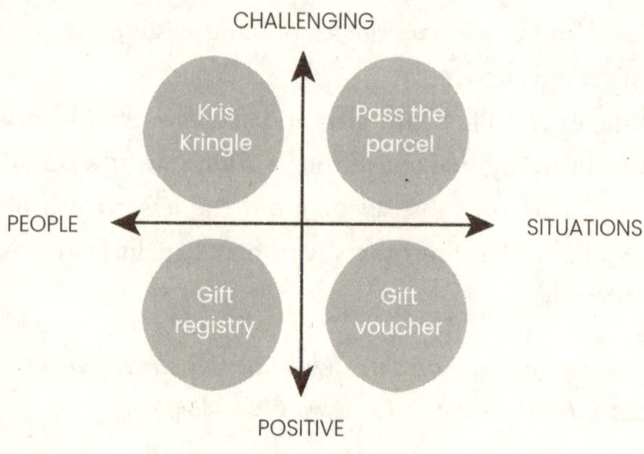

1. Pass the Parcel – challenging situations

Who doesn't remember playing Pass the Parcel as a child? In this classic British game popularised in Australia, a neatly wrapped newspaper parcel would be passed around a circle of excited kids. Each child would take their time passing it on, hoping the music stopped so they would get to remove a layer of paper to expose a small gift. You never knew who would get to open a layer and you never knew what you were going to get: a small pencil, a bar of chocolate or a plastic spider. Usually the biggest gift was in the last layer of the parcel. Now I think of it, not getting a gift in Pass the Parcel was resilience-building and having to unwrap each layer, as with our gifts in life, brought you closer to the main prize: the real gift.

In life, challenging situations are like playing Pass the Parcel. They are spontaneous and the gift in the situation is never usually planned, clear or accepted in the moment.

Two years ago my client Anna found out her daughter had cancer, which rocked her world. She resigned from a job she loved to care for her child, who has since gone into remission. Not long after this she started her own consultancy – she now has work–life balance and is doing what she loves.

This is an example of a Pass the Parcel gift: not pleasant, not chosen but it all worked out in the end. This isn't always the case, but a lesson can always be learnt from the challenging situations we face in and out of work.

2. Kris Kringle – challenging people

Certain people in our lives are the gifts that keep on giving. A Kris Kringle is a random gift, a bit like a challenging situation – you never know what is going to turn up. You may ask for a certain perfume or aftershave as your Kris Kringle present, but instead you receive a statue of an elephant. Life is as random as the people we encounter.

The challenging person can be an amazing gift that teaches us a great deal. They may be someone new in your life, in or out of work, or they may be someone you have known for a long time – maybe even a close friend or acquaintance.

In my corporate life I had a Kris Kringle manager. He never shared anything with the team, he stole ideas and he took credit for them as his own. He made work almost unbearable yet he seemed to have little awareness of the impact of his behaviour on others. As unpleasant as this situation was, it taught me a valuable lesson. The gift he gave me was knowing how *not* to be as a leader. To manage the situation, I embarked on a lot of self-development that has helped me do what I do today.

Remember that challenging, even toxic, people can be the gifts that keep on giving. Thank your Kris Kringles – they have given you some of your most valuable lessons.

3. Gift registry – positive people

In 2002 my fiancé and I excitedly scouted Myer, choosing the gifts we wanted on our marriage gift registry. It was so empowering to choose beautiful items that would serve us in life together, yet it felt surreal – like shopping for free. We still use some of these gifts to this day, and remember who gifted them all those years ago.

Positive people are similar in that you can seek them out and nurture deep and connected relationships.

Having a positive experience with certain people who contribute to your successes should be shared and not kept secret. Not sharing is like having a secret weapon and is, I believe, a selfish way to live. If you've had a great mentor or boss, share what you have learnt with others and, where you can, emulate what you liked about them. Even go so far as to share these people as a resource for the rest of your business.

Richard Branson endorses this gift regularly and credits his success to leveraging the strengths of the people around him.

Some people come to you and some you seek out – like choosing the gifts for your gift registry.

4. The gift voucher – positive situations

Similar to the gift registry, the gift voucher enables us choice. Think of receiving an iTunes voucher – you have the option to purchase music, apps or movies. We can't always seek out perfect situations as an incubator for success, but we can embrace our positive situations and successes and share these with others. When we share successes, we give hope to others and often save them from reinventing the wheel by showing what can be done.

The gift voucher may be a success you have encountered, such as nailing a big presentation to a board. It may be a personal success, such as starting a side hustle or winning a sporting final. Whatever it is for you, think about what led to that situation being successful. What helped and what hindered you?

I am blessed to be part of Thought Leaders Business School, an amazing community that shares not only the challenges but also the successes of those running a thought-leadership practice. The generosity of this community that Matt Church and Peter Cook have built is profound, and all sharing comes from a place of love, gratitude and contribution. Sharing your successes not only helps others, but also helps you to understand the process and lessons you have learned.

As we move through the 12 Gifts in the chapters to follow, think about where these gifts may be driven from – people or situations? Challenges or positive experiences?

Three

THE PATHWAY TO A GIFT MINDSET®

To move towards living the Gift Mindset, we need to understand our current position – where we sit on the path to bringing the Gift Mindset into our everyday lives. In the case of adopting a Gift Mindset, we can go from being unaware – having our gifts tightly wrapped – to being limitless as we live our legacy by unwrapping and exposing our gifts to the world.

Firstly, it is important to remember where the gifts we share can come from:

- challenges – situations or people
- positive situations or people
- personal experience outside work
- professional experience within the workplace.

The following figure represents your transformative pathway to cultivating the Gift Mindset. You might stop at five stages along the journey to adopting a Gift Mindset. How quickly you get back on the pathway depends on your awareness, acceptance and action of the gifts you encounter.

The pathway to a Gift Mindset®

INDIVIDUAL OR ORGANISATION POSITION	BEHAVIOUR	FOCUS	SUCCESS FACTOR
Legacy	Limitless	Engagement	x 10
Revealed	Fearless	Education	x 5
GIFT MINDSET® CULTURE			
Unwrapped	Courageous	Experience	x 2
Untied	Limited	Event	x 1.5
Wrapped	Unaware	Inertia	x 1

Let's take a look at each of the five steps along the pathway.

Wrapped – unaware

Focus is on inertia

At this stage, the gifts in your life are wrapped up and you are unaware that they even exist. They may be right in front of you, ready for you to open, but you aren't seeing them. Think of a Christmas tree with presents piled high underneath and then forgotten about until Christmas morning, or the hidden jewellery box gathering dust in your closet.

You may have taken one of your successes for granted or overcome a challenge or crisis and swept it into your subconscious. It could be that a person who taught you your biggest lesson, either through a positive or negative experience, hasn't made it to your conscious awareness.

Here your focus is on inertia. The odds of change are almost non-existent, with little or no thinking about what you are missing, what you could gain or what you have experienced.

When I see people at this level they are usually:

- living their life in autopilot
- not open to reflection or aware of it as an option
- time-poor
- adopting a fixed mindset
- outwardly focused.

Living at this level impacts your success and the success of others as you are not sharing your lessons.

Key questions

- Reflect – what is a gift that you haven't unwrapped?
- Was it a challenge or a success?

Untied – limited

Focus is on the event of the gift

At this stage, you see the gift as an event. It is one-dimensional; it is in your thoughts, but in a passive way. This is the start of developing the Gift Mindset – the bow may have been untied, but the wrapping is still intact.

Maybe you acknowledge a challenge that you have faced and think about it, but then dismiss it and move on. Moving forward is important, but not at the cost of acknowledging what you have learnt and how you can apply the lesson and share it. Many workplace cultures hinder our openness to share our vulnerabilities, or celebrate and share our successes. Many focus on being a transactional, performance-based culture instead – not ideal. Even our upbringing and ethnicity can play a huge part in the way in which we adopt a Gift Mindset.

Brianna was Head of People and Performance in a multinational I worked with for a few years. She achieved some amazing successes through initiatives she implemented across a plethora of divisions. She was passionate, well respected and easy to relate to, effecting positive change in the organisational culture. The day she decided to move on and explore a role abroad, she engaged me to assist in mapping out a handover strategy for her replacement. She ran me through her ideas and an induction program framework, but I was shocked to see that most of her ideas were factual. It was basically a list of *what* had been done and key initiatives she had implemented, and suggestions for future opportunities. There was nothing about *how* she had achieved success, or what had worked or failed – no roadmap for the next person to replicate success. Brianna was seeing all she had done as an event, 'the what', and was stuck at this level. We brainstormed her biggest lessons and how she could communicate these to assist the new hire. Once she delved into the lessons, she was well on her way to the next level – unwrapping the gift.

People at this level tend to think about and discuss a challenge or a success, but may shut it down. They are:

- only focused on the event – the *what*
- not open to exploring the lessons
- time-poor
- unaware of the opportunity to benefit others
- keeping their lessons to themselves.

Key questions

- Name a gift you have received, either a challenge or a success.
- What happened and what was your experience of it – why, what and how?

Unwrapped – courageous

Focus is on the experience of the gift

You are now unwrapping the gift. You've untied the bow and you're taking off the paper. You are in a whirl of thoughts as you make sense of the gift. At this stage, you are aware of what has happened – the event – and now you are in the process of raising your awareness to understand the experience.

It can take a lot of courage to unwrap the gifts we are given. Many people feel indulgent exploring a success or achieving a milestone. Many find it confronting to self-reflect or have a high benchmark for success and feel that the great things they may achieve are just part of their job or who they are.

I remember coaching a sales manager who struggled with sharing the successes he and his team had experienced. He believed they were all adults who were paid to do a job; there was no need to advertise to the world what they were achieving. The cost of this was that his tried-and-tested, best-practice examples of how success can be achieved weren't shared. In the end, his team went unrecognised for all the great work they were doing. He simply needed to reframe – sharing success was sharing the lessons to help others achieve more, as one organisation.

On the flip side, many people hide their mistakes and challenges. These are sometimes difficult to unwrap for fear of:

- reliving the event
- being seen as a failure
- not knowing how to articulate what happened.

Your success and that of others can be amplified if you have the courage to own your gifts and take the time to understand them.

Key questions

- What gift stands out for you and what were the main lessons you learnt?
- What will it cost you not to understand the experience and lesson of the gift?

Revealed – fearless

Focus is on education and understanding the gift

Think about something you have faced. Reflect on what happened and the experience of it. What did you learn? If you can easily bring something to mind and identify the learning outcome, you are probably living within the Revealed stage of cultivating the Gift Mindset.

You have developed the self-awareness to experience and understand the events that come into your life. You are fearless and you have ripped the wrapping off. The gift sparkles, revealing all it has to give, and now you need to use it to educate others.

All organisations have subject-matter experts who hold ideas and knowledge critical to the business. You may be this person and, if so, may need to think about future generations and how you can multiply the impact of what you know and what you have learnt.

This is no different from your home life – for example, sharing with your children a lesson or story that you believe will assist them. My nonna shared many authentic Italian recipes and the stories behind them with me when I was a child, from making pasta to stuffing artichokes or perfecting the best-tasting sugo. These recipes are woven into my life. What gifts are you sharing with your loved ones at home?

When sharing the gifts we have experienced, we need to make sure they are relevant to the person we're sharing with, otherwise it could come across as gloating when sharing a success or negative when sharing a challenge. At the 'Revealed' level you are able to weave your lessons (gifts) into everyday dialogue, at work or in your personal life, in a way that people can relate to and learn from.

People at this level are embracing their gifts and using them to be of greater service to self, others and the world as a whole.

They are:

- self-aware
- accepting of their gifts
- planning with whom they will share their gifts.

Key questions

- What key gifts stand out?
- Which will you share?
- Who will benefit?

Legacy – limitless

Focus is on engaging others to learn from your gifts

At this stage, you are fully living the Gift Mindset. The gift is glowing in all its glory and being received as part of who you are and what you naturally do. The Gift Mindset is a key trait of being what I call a Limitless Leader™ – one who evolves, learns and unlearns, and helps create what I call a limitless culture.

This is the living legacy level, where you are using your lessons to help others grow in and out of the workplace. This could be through conversation, stories – the eternal conduit bringing people together – or more formally through planned presentations, keynotes or mastermind sessions with your team, peers or customers. The Gift Mindset promotes openness, learning and a culture of sharing and transparency.

In your personal life, you embrace your challenges and successes and share these with family, friends and loved ones. This helps those around you to fuel their desire for success, giving them energy and motivation.

People at this level are:

- admired as an inspirational person or leader
- open to sharing the negative and positive
- receptive to gifts from others
- continuously challenging themselves and testing their limits
- reflecting on the lessons in their experiences
- looking for opportunity in failure as much as opportunity in success.

Back in my corporate life I worked for a manager living at this level. At the time I didn't appreciate the vulnerability he demonstrated. He was an open book, sharing failures – such as a restructure that ended up being the wrong choice – and successes. He encouraged us to share our successes as a team – not at an end-of-month meeting, but as part of our daily work. This enabled us to share best practice.

Even the smallest story of success or overcoming a challenge can infuse motivation. In a leadership role, when I felt awkward sharing successes and challenges, I had to remember that mighty oaks grow from little acorns. It's all about utilising that lesson and ensuring that others pass it on.

At this stage, you are living your legacy, creating future leaders and amplifying potential in those around you by living and sharing your gifts. You are known and admired for this.

Key questions

- How can I maintain and grow the Gift Mindset?
- What can I do to ensure the gifts I share are passed on?
- Who else can I educate and inspire?

Knowing where you sit on this pathway to the Gift Mindset is vital. By reading through each stage, you will get a feel for where your mindset is at.

How quickly you move up from a focus on 'inertia' to a focus on 'legacy' is your choice. The process is as important as the outcome, so ensure you embrace each stage of the journey by getting off the path to explore. It's a bit like goal-setting: it's the small steps and the process along the way that determines the outcome.

> *You do not rise to the level of your goals. You fall the level of your system.* —James Clear

The Gift Timeline

Over the years, working across many industries at all levels, I have seen what gets in the way of people adopting the Gift Mindset. In my own life, for example, losing my dad was a defining moment where I unconsciously adopted the Gift Mindset.

Moving from suppressing to expressing our lessons is vital in bringing our gifts to life. The following Gift Timeline shows us the two key drivers that determine where our gifts lie:

1. our level of awareness of the gift
2. our willingness to express the gift to ourselves and others.

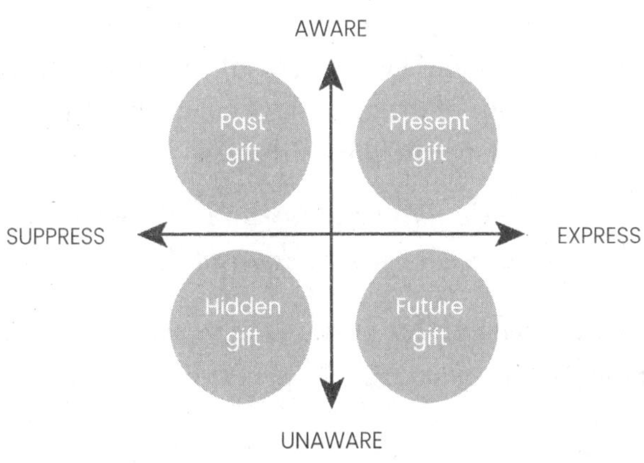

Past gifts

These are the gifts that were never opened and have been put away in the cupboard. These gifts, which could contain valuable items, remain in the past, gathering dust. Past gifts normally come about when we are suppressing the lesson they hold, even though we are aware of it. Maybe we don't want to deal with what happened, or we don't see the lesson as valuable. Suppression could also be due to being time-poor and distracted with life. Remember, the past is about learning and the future is about progress.

Tip: Think about something that has happened in your past that may assist you and others now.

Hidden gifts

You have low or no awareness of these, making it hard to identify them – although others around you may see them. This is where ongoing feedback and disclosure is important. Hidden gifts might be in your past, or right in front of you in the present moment.

Tip: Ask trusted friends or colleagues if they have observed a success or challenge you may have missed.

Future gifts

The event that will trigger a future gift has either not yet occurred, or is in the process of happening. Your awareness may be low while you are living it, but it may be visible to others. As time progresses, you will move into one of the other three quadrants, depending on your self-awareness and expression of the gift.

Tip: Keep being in the moment and invest in self-reflective time and activities to be present in what you are experiencing.

> *The future depends on what we do in the present.*
> —Mahatma Gandhi

Present gifts

These gifts are sparkling in all their glory right now. They are unwrapped and your mindset is playing out at the top two levels of the pathway to a Gift Mindset. You are self-aware and can express the lessons clearly. You share the gifts with your team, your peers, your manager and people outside work. What is important here is to maintain awareness and openness to the gifts.

Tip: Continue to share and evaluate the benefits of the Gift Mindset.

As you read this book, be open to gifts you may have in each of the four quadrants.

By identifying where your gifts sit on the Gift Timeline, you will raise your awareness and cultivate the seeds to continue to discover and share your gifts. Whether they are past, present, hidden or future, they all deserve to be unwrapped, experienced and shared at some point.

Walking the pathway to the Gift Mindset requires us to make self-reflection a priority. We can't take action unless we have awareness. This book should be regularly referred to, marked up and dirty. It should be shared, copied and discussed. A great sign of learning and progress is a worn-out book, each page provoking thought, action, debate and new ways of thinking and working.

Review your position and where those gifts may be on the timeline. Look at this book a bit like a meal: understanding your current position is like an entrée that gets your tastebuds going. As your appetite increases, you will be ready to devour the main course – unwrapping the 12 Gifts.

Four

BARRIERS TO A GIFT MINDSET®

We need to be aware of the many barriers that can prevent us from adopting the Gift Mindset so we are ready to tackle them if they appear. Barriers are the enemy of success – being mindful of them is imperative.

The following figure shows the seven key barriers I have witnessed, both in and out of a work environment, that can hinder sharing valuable lessons. There are many more, but you will get the gist. We'll then take a look at each of these in turn.

Seven key barriers to a Gift Mindset

1. Suppressed gifts
2. Judgement from others
3. Using success as a secret weapon
4. Distraction
5. Workplace culture
6. Low self-awareness
7. Lack of time and headspace

Barrier 1 – suppressed gifts

As babies, we connect naturally to our physical and emotional bodies – we are well versed in expressing our feelings. As we grow older, we develop our vocabulary, use language and learn how to read and write. We have our own thoughts and we turn to abstract concepts and words to represent our experiences. Before long we discover that when we face challenges, we can escape feelings by hiding our own thoughts. The tangible aspect of logic can allow it to be a refuge when things get messy.

All of us have had times or situations in our lives where we suppress what's really going on and internalise it. Suppression is usually ineffective over the long term, and can quickly become a coping mechanism that we default to.

When we fail to uncover, accept and express our lessons, we also fail to share them. Some of the reasons this can happen include lack of awareness, inability to articulate what we have learnt and uncertainty about who we should share it with. We can also suppress things that remind us of previous experiences or memories. For example, say Mary was your enemy at school and all memories of her make your stomach turn. When you meet someone with the name Mary many years later, you might feel uncomfortable, avoid this person (who isn't even the real enemy) and suppress this event. This is an example of activating an unwanted emotional memory that will make you either avoid similar situations or suppress the feeling itself.

We really need to move from *suppressing* our gifts to experiencing a state of *distress*, where we may feel anxiety, sorrow and even pain if the gift has come from a challenging situation or person. Once we deal with this, we can *digest* and understand the gift through reflection, which in turn increases our self-awareness and acceptance. Then, and only then, are we ready to *express* it.

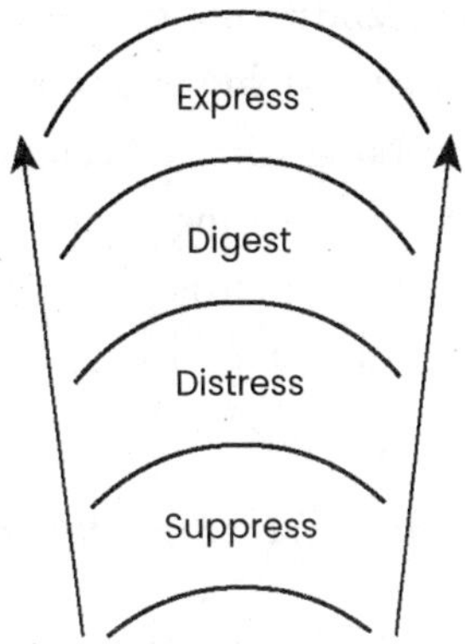

Any experience can be made into a further blockage or can become a way of freeing ourselves. —Trungpa Rinpoche

Barrier 2 – judgement from others

Many people feel it's not their place to share their lessons.

In a recent discussion with a group of clients, many said they felt self-indulgent sharing successes. They said they felt as if they were gloating and that their team would see them as egotistical. You may agree, but remember this is only the frame that you are viewing the situation through. Your belief that sharing success is egotistical is larger than your desire to share and replicate success. Your 'why' to change this belief needs to become bigger than your 'why' to stay the same. If you can relate to this, take the time to flip your belief and focus on the potential benefits sharing your successes could bring.

Failing to share your successes and challenges is selfish.

If you're willing to have a go at sharing a small or large success, start by looking at where you have come from and the lessons (gifts) that have enabled you. The most effective leaders are the ones who overcome adversity by planting positive seeds, feeding them with optimistic energy and then watching success grow.

A team I've been working with has started 'Win Wednesdays', where they kick off the day sharing a win or success and how it came to be (the lesson). This can foster an open and sharing culture across the organisation, ultimately leading to higher morale and performance.

Your darkest moments can be those that define you.

Sometimes people feel inadequate sharing challenges they have faced or mistakes they have made. They feel judged and anxious about the response they will receive, fearing rejection. They are coming from a place of fear, rather than a place of love. We share more with those we trust, respect and have rapport with on a personal level, and this can be mirrored in the workplace if we foster these traits.

We need to embrace our challenges and welcome sharing these. All challenges are vital to our personal development. The more we test our capabilities and limits, the more we will learn about ourselves. If we focus on what it would be like to fail, and therefore revert to our comfort zone, there will be no growth.

I encourage organisations I work with to embed 'Win Wednesday' as well as:

- 'Motivation Monday' – sharing what lights you up
- 'Failure Friday' – sharing challenges and discussing the lessons learnt.

Making an event of sharing creates a sense of fun and theatre, and a safe space to be open and own your experiences as a team.

One way to motivate others and make sharing successes and challenges routine practice is to explore positive-to-negative ratios. Psychologist John Gottman researched this and found 5:1 to be the 'magic ratio', where five positive mentions or moments are shared for every negative one. Another study showed that teams with a positive-to-negative ratio greater than 3:1 were significantly more motivated.

Remember that our expectations can create our reality and the stereotypes we hold can impact our behaviour. Psychologists call this process 'stereotype threat'.

Imagine you are running a session at a senior leadership team meeting for the first time. Your manager has stressed the importance of getting it right, and the potential impact on your leadership brand, team and so on. You are aware of being the 'new kid on the block' so you're anxious about potentially making a mistake. Your manager even introduces you by reinforcing this is the first time you have presented at this level. You get distracted from your focus on presenting effectively and focus instead on the technology not working, not coming across clearly or having your message diluted by nerves. This demonstrates how stereotypes can impact our behaviour. So, if we place concern on a situation such as a culture that doesn't encourage sharing of success and/or challenges, we are confirming a negative stereotype. This will disrupt our ability to focus on a particular task that will lead to adopting a Gift Mindset.

The key is to keep the sharing truthful and honest. This encourages positive emotions, and can have a healthy ripple effect across the organisation.

Barrier 3 – using success as a secret weapon

In any business, we need to be successful to survive. We learn vicariously through the experiences of others by way of innovation, optimism, problem-solving and finding new opportunities, in conjunction with personal development and experience. Sharing our experiences is vital.

Unfortunately, many people choose to use their successes as a 'secret weapon' – they hide their personal or team successes and how they achieved them, failing to share and promote them within the organisation. The reasons they do this are usually unspoken – not wanting to share what they think belongs to them, a fear that others may take their role, or that they will be copied and therefore not stand out. These reasons are all fear-based but, sadly, exist in many organisations.

'Keeping up with the Joneses' means using our neighbours as a benchmark. To many, failing to keep up with the Joneses is perceived as demonstrating socioeconomic or cultural inferiority. In many social circles people share their successes, but not how they achieved them, in order to have a competitive advantage – similar to the workplace. This is the opposite of having a Gift Mindset, which is all about sharing best practice so others can replicate success.

People can also be a secret weapon. Many years ago, I finished a 12-month one-on-one mentoring program with a senior sales manager. It went well, and I asked if he could refer me to the learning and development team to explore further work within the organisation. He replied that I was his 'secret weapon': he wanted me to work only with him and his team, and didn't want to share me with the rest of the organisation. At the time this shocked me, as this is against what I believe in. Not long after this he came around, and I worked throughout the organisation.

All over the world, organisations know the importance of learning, and therefore invest heavily in formal in-house and external training, mentoring programs and systems to manage the sharing of experiences. It is staggering that analysts estimate that the companies in the Fortune 500 still lose a combined $31 billion per year from employees failing to share knowledge effectively. This has a direct impact on productivity within the organisation. People waste time and resources by reinventing the wheel, reliving the mistakes of others and wasting time researching solutions and information to create future success.

> *If only HP knew what HP knows, we would be three times more productive.* —Lew Platt, former CEO, Hewlett-Packard

What will it cost you and those around you *not* to share your successes, or what you may call your secret weapons?

Barrier 4 – distraction

> *Never in human history have our brains had to work with so much information as they do today … We have a generation of people who are so busy processing the information received from all directions that they are losing the ability to think and feel.*
> —Edward Hallowell, US psychiatrist

When we are distracted we can become removed from the present moment. We are not as open to what is going on around us, which leads to a lack of focus on what is important. This can stifle our ability to think and feel, as we lose connection to ourselves and others. This can lead to limited disclosure, a lack of deep and meaningful relationships and interactions and, ultimately, isolation.

Not only does distraction lower our productivity and energy, but it affects our ability to focus on and stick with projects. It affects our mindset – that is, our beliefs, thoughts and expectations that will determine how we perceive and therefore respond to what happens to us. Every day we are bombarded with more information than we can process. From scrolling through our social media feeds to reading the newspaper, turning on the television and radio or simply surfing the internet, we attempt to make sense of all the data being directed at us.

It's impossible to process everything that is thrown at us, let alone make the time to adopt and apply the Gift Mindset.

To combat this information overload, we tend to take shortcuts in our thinking, expectations and problem-solving, usually unconsciously. Often these shortcuts are based on stereotypes formed by our experiences, reinforced by the media. A simple mental shortcut could be assuming we can't be an effective public speaker because so many around us dread it. Outside work, you may believe the more expensive washing machine will produce cleaner clothes than the less expensive model, when in fact both will do the job. Your assumption that more expensive is better is a shortcut to your buying decisions in this case. These mental shortcuts can block us from the truth of both our assumptions and our mindset.

In a 2018 Udemy for Business survey, nearly three out of four workers (70%) admitted they feel distracted at work, with 16% of people stating that they're almost always distracted.

The impact of workplace distractions, according to the report, included that:

- 54% said they 'aren't performing as well as they should'
- 50% said they 'are significantly less productive'
- 20% said they are 'not able to reach full potential and advance in their career'.

The same survey from Udemy cited the top benefits of reducing workplace distraction from those interviewed:

- 75% stated 'I get more done and I'm more productive'
- 57% stated 'I'm motivated to do my best'
- 51% stated 'I'm more confident in my ability to do my job well'
- 49% stated 'I'm happier at work'
- 44% stated 'I deliver higher quality work'.

Top distractions included talkative co-workers (cited by 80% of workers surveyed), and office noise (70%).

Meetings were blamed for low productivity by 60% of respondents, while 58% said that, although they don't need social media to do their jobs, they couldn't make it through the working day without checking platforms such as Facebook, Twitter and Instagram.

Distractions can come in many forms. Out of work, household chores may prevent you from doing what lights you up, or taking reflective time to self-develop or exercise. At work, it may be the talkative person you sit next to, emails, meetings, noisy surroundings, unclear expectations, a thankless boss or scrolling through Facebook or LinkedIn.

When our main goal is to avoid discomfort, we can get caught up in what is comfortable, and this can disconnect us from ourselves and others.

Living in the age of distraction, we need to make time to do what matters instead of serving the distractors around us. Doing the right thing at the right time for the right results should be your focus, and living the Gift Mindset is a part of this.

Barrier 5 – workplace culture

Culture is the shared beliefs, values, customs and social behaviour of a community. Many organisational cultures do not encourage or condone the sharing of challenges or failures and successes. This means that sharing might never enter your mind, especially if your current organisation is all you have ever known.

This is the same at home. If you are brought up to just suck it up and get on with things, chances are this behaviour will play out in your life. On the flip side, if you are encouraged to share successes and challenges at home, at school and within your social network, you will be more open to the Gift Mindset.

Not everyone works in an organisation that is open to the idea of being reflective. When management doesn't see reflective practice as important, being open to sharing your lessons can go by the wayside. I come across enough companies like this to know the challenges faced by people within them who want an open, self-reflective and sharing culture.

> *You must be the change you want to see in the world.*
> —Mahatma Gandhi

Start small. Maybe initiate some of the activities outlined earlier in this chapter at certain team catch-ups. Maximise online platforms such as Yammer and Office 365 Teams to create the space for sharing. Cultural change takes time – it starts with the people.

Comfort and fear are the enemies of progress

One way to gradually change a culture to adopt the Gift Mindset is by shadowing and sharing best practice of success, and lessons learnt from challenges. This can also be done by not just talking and/or observing someone, but also encouraging interactive conversation and questioning. This allows the learner to understand the reasons behind someone else's actions, making it easier to adapt what's learned to a new situation or task.

One study found that pharmaceutical development teams were better able to translate and learn from another team's past experience when they invited members of the other team – the 'sharers' of knowledge – to actively participate in their discussion and problem-solving, rather than the 'learner' team simply identifying the 'sharer' team's knowledge and then trying to replicate it on their own.

Barrier 6 – low self-awareness

Self-awareness is simply awareness of all of the elements that make up our unique identity. Psychologist Daniel Goleman defined self-awareness in his best-selling book *Emotional Intelligence* as 'knowing one's internal states, preferences, resources, and intuitions'.

When somebody is lacking self-awareness, they are lacking the ability to monitor their inner world, their emotions and their thoughts. It is important to note that self-awareness is not just what we notice about ourselves, but also what we observe and monitor about our outer world.

Self-awareness is the cornerstone to emotional intelligence (EI), and the more we can tap into and understand our inner world, the more we can foster the Gift Mindset. If we are unaware of the events we experience, chances are the lessons we have learnt will be difficult to decipher.

If self-awareness is so important, why aren't we more self-aware? Most commonly, we lack being present; we are simply 'not there' to observe ourselves or pay attention to what's going on inside or around us.

Psychologists Matthew Killingsworth and Daniel T Gilbert found that almost half of the time we operate on 'automatic pilot' – we are unconscious of what we are doing or how we feel, as our mind wanders somewhere else.

Creating space for yourself and jealously protecting this can help you focus on being present. Keep a journal and capture your thoughts and feelings. Even if you never read what you write again, you have externalised your thoughts and feelings, which will help you to be more in the moment. This has helped me as I find it extremely hard to be still and not think ahead, therefore missing what is happening in the moment.

Mastering your listening skills can also assist with ramping up your self-awareness. Listening is about being present and paying attention to other people's emotions, body movement and language. It is about showing empathy and understanding without constantly evaluating or coming from a place of judgement. It is also about listening to what is *not* being said when interacting face to face. It is well known that words only account for 7% of the message, with body language and tone, pitch and pace accounting for up to 93% of the overall message. By becoming an effective listener, you will also be better at listening to your own inner voice and become your own best friend.

Awareness is the first step of adopting a Gift Mindset and what happens next builds on it.

It still holds true that man is most uniquely human when he turns obstacles into opportunities. —Eric Hoffer

Barrier 7 – lack of time and headspace

In today's world, fewer people are doing more, both inside and outside work, and this often sets an unrealistic expectation of what can be achieved. This leaves many people feeling unmotivated, unfulfilled and therefore feeling guilty about what is *not* being achieved, rather than acknowledging what *is*.

Many of us lack time to embrace what we have experienced and learnt from in life. We go from point A to point B almost on autopilot, looking for the next shiny thing. When time is a barrier to adopting the Gift Mindset, this has a direct impact on our self-awareness.

Your actions and results stem directly from how effectively or ineffectively you manage yourself.

I'm a believer in self-management, not time management. Time is inelastic; we are all given the same amount and need to manage ourselves in order to maximise it.

In any typical 8-hour workday, we are given 32 sets of 15-minute blocks – that equates to 160 opportunities a week to set aside 25 minutes to work on our Gift Mindset.

Being time-poor is the biggest challenge I see and hear about at all levels of leadership across varying industries. As a person who leverages the hell out of every minute, I believe your success in managing yourself comes down to being aware of two key things: headspace and energy. In order to lead and serve ourselves, our teams and our organisations, we need to do the right things at the right time. What we let into our headspace will affect our energy, so be mindful of what you are doing and also what you are thinking. For example, if you get home from work and keep thinking about the day that was and the next big presentation coming up, that's going to affect your headspace – and, more importantly, how you are at home. This internal chatter consumes your thoughts, then flows into your energy.

Neuroscientist Paul MacLean came up with the well-known model of brain structure and how it relates to function in the 1960s. His 'triune brain' model is based on three dominant structures in the human brain – the reptilian brain, the monkey brain and the logical brain. It has been found since that the three structures do not operate independently, but influence one another via numerous interconnections.

In a nutshell:

- The reptilian brain's primary focus is to survive. This brain kicks in if you are under pressure or faced with a threat that causes a fight-or-flight response.
- The monkey brain, or relationship brain, can become easily distracted – its main focus is to look for connection. This brain is the one that may struggle to focus on one thing, cause internal chatter and trigger self-doubt. It is simply the noise in our heads; the cheeky, disruptive brain that takes you off course and tempts you with thoughts and inner dialogue that do not serve you.
- The logical brain – our leadership brain – is the one that looks into the future. Its key role is to think about and create a better world. It also assists us to solve problems creatively. This is where I believe successful people operate from. Sounds easy? Not at all; this is a constant battle for most people.

By being aware of how our brain works, we can consciously know where we are operating from. Our thoughts are the only thing we can control – the payoff from the time, focus and laser-like discipline this requires is huge.

So, take time to control the monkey brain and don't buy into its chatter. Listen to your negative inner dialogue and flip it. What unresolved situations are you carrying around to muddy the clarity of your world? What thoughts are going around in circles that you are 'awfulising' (think downward-spiralling thoughts)?

By being self-aware, you can prevent the reptilian brain from kicking in and triggering that fight-or-flight response. If you want to adopt the Gift Mindset, you must manage yourself in order to manage your time and what you are focusing on. Delegate more, plan and protect your time and, above all, make the space for self-reflection.

Being aware of these seven barriers to living with a Gift Mindset empowers you to take hold of them and minimise them so you stay focused and aware. Failing to see the obstacles to having a Gift Mindset is like forgetting to lay the foundation of a house. You can continue to build the house, but the outcome will never be as robust or last the test of time.

What barriers do you need to bust through? Make a note of these and write down two actionable points for each that you can implement to eradicate these barriers to the Gift Mindset.

Five

HOW TO ADOPT A GIFT MINDSET®

So far, we have looked into what the Gift Mindset is, why it matters and the key drivers. We have explored the timeline of gifts and looked at cultivating this mindset and the barriers that stand in our way. Knowing something is only half the equation, though; *doing* is where change happens. Now we are ready to unwrap the 'how' of adopting the Gift Mindset.

Unwrapping your gifts – the three As

The process consists of three main steps:

1. creating awareness of the event
2. accepting the experience
3. acting on the lessons.

By creating awareness, we can take the time needed to reflect, unwrap the gift and see the opportunity. Acceptance is where we reframe the event as an experience and accept it to help us and others, rather than resist it and let it hinder us. Then we can take action to bring the lessons to life and help others to grow.

Let's break down the process so you can apply it within a framework.

Step 1 – Awareness

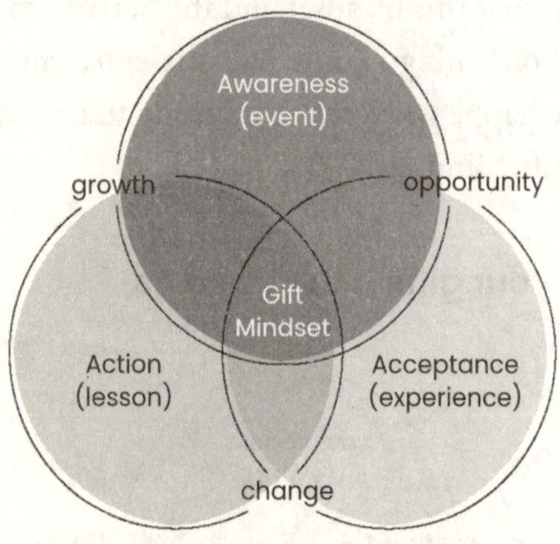

From the ancient Greek saying 'know thyself' to Western psychology, self-awareness has been studied throughout the ages.

Whether facing a challenge or a success, the first step in adopting the Gift Mindset is to have deeper awareness of what happened (the event). Failing to do this leaves the event one-dimensional. Imagine this as a fully wrapped-up gift. A crisis, success or challenge can send us into a tornado of confusion, denial and sometimes defeat. By going through the 'unwrapping' process, we can peel back the layers and see the gift in a way that serves us and others.

Emotional intelligence

As we explored in chapter 4, people with high awareness are usually high in emotional intelligence (EI); they have the ability to recognise, understand and monitor the emotions of self and others. EI was named in the early 1990s by Peter Salovey and John D Mayer, and many psychologists since then have agreed on four key qualities of emotionally intelligent people:

1. self-awareness
2. self-management
3. social awareness
4. social skills.

> *If your emotional abilities aren't in hand, if you don't have self-awareness, if you are not able to manage your distressing emotions, if you can't have empathy and have effective relationships, then no matter how smart you are, you're not going to get very far.* —Daniel Goleman

EI remains a standout skill in both leadership and life, in many cases surpassing technical ability and overall IQ. A 2011 CareerBuilder survey of 2600 hiring managers and leaders came up with some standout findings:

- 71% stated they valued EI over IQ
- 75% were more likely to promote a highly emotionally intelligent worker
- 59% said they would pass on a candidate with high IQ and low EI.

and *citta* means 'heart' or 'mind'. This practice will open you up to adopting the Gift Mindset and being able to bring benefits, lessons and inspiration to others.

Bodhicitta requires learning everything about our own heart and mind. Through reading, meditation, ramping up our EI and questioning our experiences, we can become more present.

Many people try to go around, not through, a challenge or crisis. Cutting through helps us to learn from the experience. We need to be open to both our successes and challenges – gifts lie within both.

Take the time to reflect on situations – the people involved, what happened and how it made you feel – not just logically, but in your heart and your body.

> *Any experience can be made into a further blockage or can become a way of freeing ourselves.* —Trungpa Rinpoche

Triad of multifaceted awareness

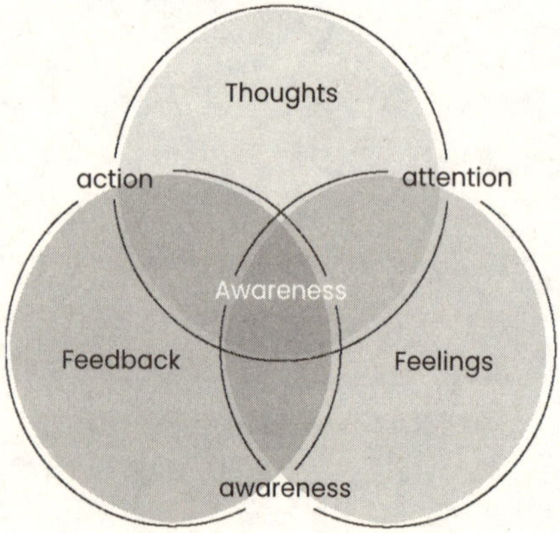

When we take our thoughts, feelings and feedback from the outside world into consideration, we have multifaceted awareness. Let's look at the three key components.

1. Thoughts

The mind is powerful and your thoughts are the starting point to awareness and where your attention goes.

Brain science has given us insights into what is known as 'neuroplasticity'. Buddhism has a similar concept – planting karmic seeds. This means that each of our actions and thoughts sows seeds in our subconscious that will eventually grow and come to fruition.

An example could be thinking someone at work has it in for you – they seem to look at you strangely and avoid you. Soon, your thoughts become your reality – you start to pick out that person's shortcomings. In fact, this person could have a whole range of reasons for 'avoiding' you: they could be under pressure, shy, or even believe that *you* are avoiding *them*.

Our thoughts dictate our feelings and what we action or avoid.

Our inner voice narrates our lives; its monologue has enormous power over us. Negative self-talk can include:

- **awfulising** – assuming the worst; this can spiral into negative thinking
- **filtering** – seeing only the negative aspects when you face a challenge, although positive aspects exist in parallel
- **personalising** – blaming yourself when faced with a challenge.

The thoughts you think today will determine the results you see tomorrow. —Robin Sharma

If you are finding that your inner voice is persistently negative, you might like to try the following tips:

- **Catch your critic and name it:** Stop and name the thought and then refer to it by that name. One of my clients attributed inner talk about not being good enough to 'needy Ned'.

like and need feedback. Many senior leaders I come across tend to be internally focused, especially if they have been in a role for a long time. They rely on their intuition rather than seeking feedback from others. The danger of this is that they can become blinded to opportunity, and miss out on feedback that could be helpful.

Ensure you give people feedback the way they like it – some people like a lot of feedback and some like it less often; some prefer to be given feedback privately versus publicly.

Journalling for self-awareness

Many of my clients use journalling to work through the triad of self-acceptance – they find it helpful to put their thoughts and memories of an event down on paper. Here are some questions you can work through:

- **Thoughts:**
  - Was the event a success, a challenge or a crisis?
  - What happened and what did you tell yourself?
  - What were your beliefs around this?
- **Feelings:**
  - How did it make you feel?
  - Did you respond or react to the event?
  - How did you manage your feelings?
- **Outside feedback:**
  - What feedback did you receive or notice?
  - What was happening outside you?
  - How were others around you reacting/responding?
  - What were you seeing and hearing?

Awareness takes time

For many of us, self-awareness is something we need to continually work at. We need to give ourselves the time and space needed to process our thoughts and become aware of how we are feeling, as well as seek feedback from others to help us understand what's going on for us.

In March 2019 I was driving to visit a regional client when my beautiful sister phoned to tell me she had been diagnosed with breast cancer. I reacted at first with shock, sadness and, understandably, not too many words. Then, during the two-hour drive, I took the time to reflect on the news that had rocked my world.

Firstly, I thought about my sister's long track record of ill health and misfortunes. I thought about how strong her mindset has been, and will continue to be, to conquer this terrible disease. As I kept thinking these thoughts, although still devastated I felt lighter, better able to deal with the situation, more in control. From outside, I heard that my family and friends were in shock. The doctors had formulated a treatment plan and were positive that my sister had every chance of beating the disease. I took notice of all this, along with my own thoughts and feelings, to make sense of the situation. I hadn't accepted it yet, but I was aware of what I was thinking, how I was feeling and what was going on around me.

Being stuck in the car gave me the time and space to process my initial feelings and thoughts, allowing me to begin to move forward and support my sister. Sometimes we're not that lucky – crises often happen at busy moments when we're not able to slow down. That's why it's so important to deliberately plan space and time into our weeks to foster self-awareness.

You can't adopt the Gift Mindset without continually working on your self-awareness. By doing so, you increase the likelihood of uncovering the potential gift, and seeing what it can offer you and others.

self-compassion in. Self-compassion researcher Kristin Neff highlights its many benefits, including a decrease in anxiety, stress and depression, and an increase in life satisfaction, resilience and overall happiness.

I have many amazing friends and, until recently, couldn't name a time that I had fallen out with any of them. Then a close friend threw me under a bus to protect herself from having to take the blame for something. We had grown up together and the situation, plus the fact that she never apologised, really played on me. I realised that even if the threads of our friendship were salvaged, our values didn't align anymore. Although we speak in passing and there is no animosity, things will never be the same.

I used a three-step process called CAN to get through this situation, because I recognised that my self-compassion needed to be ramped up. CAN opens the door to what is possible when you focus on self-acceptance or self-compassion. The CAN process employs 'illeism' – the act of referring to oneself in the third person. Studies have shown that when people use illeism to talk about traumatic events or challenges, they tend to regard themselves through more compassionate eyes. This disassociation is useful in diluting the pain. CAN works like this:

- **C – Confess to the pain or event.** What is happening?

  This is where you need to clearly state the pain or challenge you are facing.

  'Renée is feeling hurt and hard done by.'

- **A – Align.** Who else may feel this or be experiencing this?

  When we associate what we are going through as a common, shared experience, we tend to feel more settled and calm. It's almost like this soothes us and gets us to focus our attention outward. It is known that our brain's social-care circuit primes itself with oxytocin in social situations that make us feel supported and connected with others.

'Renée is not the only one experiencing this. Many people feel hurt and have gone through a similar experience.'

- **N – Nourish.** What can I do or think that will serve me resourcefully?

  By reassuring yourself in the third person, you offer yourself useful advice. At this stage you could even come up with an affirmation. In the scenario I've shared, I only have to remind myself of how many amazing people I have in my life to remember the compassion and respect I have for myself, which dictates who I let in to my life.

  'Renée has been through harder things. Time heals all and she just needs to focus on the amazing people in her life.'

Resist or embrace?

Once we have harnessed self-compassion, we have a choice. Do we embrace the positive or challenging experience and accept it, or do we resist and fight against it?

The following diagram shows the choices we all have access to, in order to embrace or resist the experiences we go through from a people or situational perspective.

Maybe you have experienced a success such as turning your side hustle into a lucrative enterprise. You may feel embarrassed, almost egotistical, to share your story, so you resist sharing the experience and what, and who, helped you get there. It is important to remember that we resist sharing not only challenges, but also successes – and this can hinder us.

Embracing positive people and situations can lead to our life's highlights. On the flip side, if we resist or repel the experience or person we can feel helpless, and this can hinder us as outlined in the diagram. Resisting can make the situation even more painful and exhausting. Imagine playing a game of tug of war: you are gripping on to the rope not wanting to let go, and at the same time

Eliminate distraction

Distraction, as we noted earlier, is the perfect shield to ignore and miss the gifts we are faced with. To create a 'yes' state of mind and be open to acceptance, jot down the distractions around you. This could include certain people, thoughts, technology, unnecessary meetings or streaming Netflix whenever your mind races. You need to be aware of what gets in the way in order to open the space for the amazing process of acceptance.

Know your drivers

Motivation fuels action and this drives our behaviour. For example, if you attend meetings with a colleague who pushes your buttons, you can resist them and become bitter and vulnerable to their actions. On the flip side, you could practise calmness and learn from them. By embracing the relationship, accepting it for what it is and changing the way you interact with this person, the experience will change. Be in control of what is driving you – don't let it control you.

Just start

Perfectionism, procrastination and distraction are behaviours that can hold us back. As Lynne Cazaly outlines in her book *ish*:

> *Perfectionism is on the rise and it has dire consequences for how we think and feel about ourselves and others, how we think, live, and work. Perfectionism has been seen to cause over-thinking, over-working, burnout, sleeplessness, and mental health problems like depression and anxiety.*

Ask yourself: what is the one thing you can do to work towards embracing the experience you are facing?

Choose one thing you can change or do differently that will take you from a 'no' state to a 'yes' state, where you can say 'yes' to your current situation and your feelings, and learn to be with what you are experiencing.

As a passionate cook, I look at resisting or embracing a situation as the recipe for either success or disaster. Each recipe involves specific ingredients that make up the finished dish. Reflect on the ingredients below and see what dish you're creating.

Recipe of resistance	Recipe of acceptance
Ingredients:	*Ingredients:*
Negativity	Self-compassion
Anxiety	Expansion
Heaviness	Love
Procrastination	Freedom
Doubt	Accountability
Regret	Contribution
Distraction	Peace
Anger	Calmness
Busyness	Lightness
Blame	Confidence
Low self-awareness	Courage

My Gift of Acceptance

In December 2018, my husband and I finally called it quits after five years of trying to conceive a baby through IVF.

After many attempts, we ended up exploring the option of a donor egg thanks to a friend sharing her successful experience. We started the process, but after several FaceTime sessions with a well-known doctor in Greece, it just didn't feel right. At one stage the clinic was going to be closed when I needed to be there for the best chance of conception, and after a few late-night chats Brett and I decided it felt too forced and clinical. We pulled the pin.

Lessons shared can become your legacy to the people and organisation you serve.

A few questions to ponder:

- What lessons have you gleaned and how will you apply these?
- Who could benefit from your gifts?
- What is one thing you could do today to share a gift?

The power of story

Storytelling is a great way to share your experiences. The practice goes back to ancient times across most cultures. Parts of our brain actually light up when we hear stories. Research has shown that people are more likely to remember your message if you deliver it through a story than if you walked through hard data and statistics.

Stanford University academic Chip Heath describes an activity in which he asked students to present a speech with one story and three statistics in it. Of all the listeners, only 5% remembered a single statistic, and up to 63% remembered the story.

Here are my tips on crafting your gift as a story, whether formally or informally:

- Run through the story like a script in your head, or write it down for a more formal sharing.
- Set the scene – the why, what and how.
- Choose the right person/s to share it with.
- In three to five key steps, articulate what you did to overcome the challenge or achieve the success.
- Know the relevance of the story and why it is important to the receiver.
- Articulate the main lessons that the receiver can apply.
- Include a mini conclusion that sums up the benefit of the above.

In a work environment, you may share the lessons from your gifts in many ways. It could be as a story, an informal conversation or a more formal presentation. You may share it with internal stakeholders or your clients, if relevant.

Outside of work, you may share your gifts with a child sitting around a campfire, with a friend on the way to the footy or with your life partner. My mum often shares her experiences with me when she feels they are relevant and helpful.

There are no rules except that we *do* need to share our gifts for the greater good of those around us. Never has it been more important to focus on deeper and more meaningful connections as a human race.

Lastly, when sharing or actioning your gifts, make sure they are:

- real
- relevant
- relatable
- intentional
- in service to others.

This book is intended to be a reminder and reference point for you to continue to share and encourage others to adopt the same mindset.

As you unwrap each of the 12 Gifts in the following chapters, get ready to immerse yourself in real-life stories, interviews, tools and insights. In each chapter, we will explore key insights into each gift and give questions to enable you to reflect and act.

Just as importantly, take the time to bring your own gifts to life, returning to the ideas and processes outlined in chapters 1 to 5.

How to unwrap the gifts

Look at unwrapping the 12 Gifts like opening a box of chocolates to find individually foiled treats waiting to be unwrapped and enjoyed. Some provide certainty and some will be an unknown surprise and learning experience.

I encourage you to devote a journal to capturing your experience. Give yourself space and time to express yourself and be present. For me, a mix of pen and paper and technology such as Evernote works well. I feel more present, creative and less distracted when I have a dedicated journal I can touch, feel and access when needed. Go with whatever works for you – dogeared pages with notes, highlighted text and worn-out edges are the signs of a book that has been brought to life.

Start with any chapter – choose what you need for where you are at. What gift is most relevant to open and unwrap right now? Read through the chapter and then utilise the ideas, questions and processes offered throughout.

Layer 1 – Untie the bow

Take the time to reflect:

1. What type of gift are you unwrapping? (Refer to 'The four drivers of a Gift Mindset' in chapter 2.)

- Pass the parcel – challenging situation
- Kris Kringle – challenging person
- Gift registry – positive person
- Gift voucher – positive situation

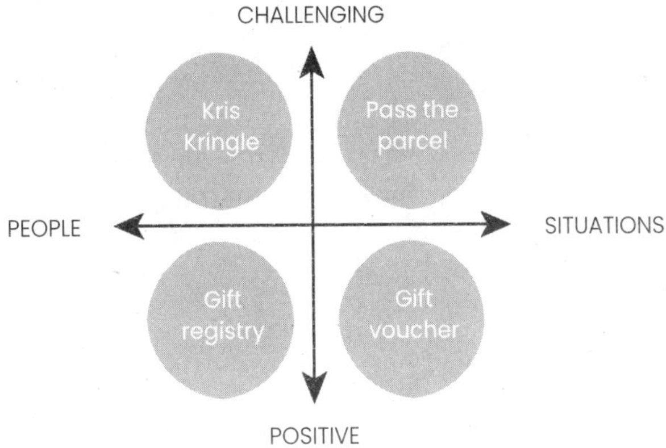

2. Where is your gift on the Gift Timeline? (Refer to chapter 3.)
    - Hidden
    - Past
    - Present
    - Future

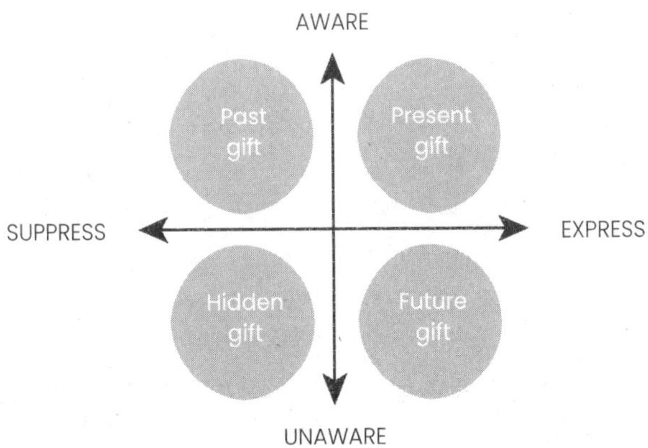

The first two steps are about you and the last two steps are about others. Here are the questions to ask yourself:

G Grow

- What key lessons has the gift taught you?
- In what ways has it helped you to learn and grow?

I Integrate

- How will you incorporate these lessons into your life moving forward?
- What do you need to be aware of and what could get in the way of you actioning these lessons?

F Facilitate

- What lessons from this gift can you share with others professionally or personally?
- Who will you share these with and how will you share this gift?

T Transform

- How will you know that this gift has transformed you and others?
- When will you share this gift with others?

Bomboniera

A 'bomboniera' is a keepsake that hosts give to their guests at weddings, baptisms and the like as a gesture of thanks. It's a memento to remember a special occasion long after it has occurred.

From my childhood, I remember the delicate little gifts of five sugar-coated almonds that lasted long after the celebrations we attended. The five almonds traditionally represent happiness, health, wealth, longevity and fertility. At my own wedding, each guest received a candle encased in a crystal glass engraved with their name, which lit up their place at the table. Along with this, they got to take home an exquisite mouth-blown Egyptian perfume bottle that I still see in friends' and family houses, capturing a moment in time.

As you complete your unwrapping of the Gift Mindset, my bomboniera for you in the following chapters is five key takeaways from each of the 12 Gifts. Refer to these as a reminder to continue to adopt and live the Gift Mindset.

Seven

THE GIFT OF OPTIMISM

When it rains, look for rainbows.
When it's dark, look for stars.
—Oscar Wilde

In this chapter, we will explore optimism and what it takes to bring this into our lives, both in and out of the workplace.

We will then unwrap:

- the impact of optimism on our health and wellbeing
- the four stages to optimism
- six keys to optimism
- the GIFT process to help you unwrap your Gift of Optimism and share it.

Let's kick off with some amazing insights extracted from an interview I did with Victor Perton, Chief Optimism Officer of Melbourne's Centre for Optimism – a movement fostering 'realistic and infectiously optimistic leaders to be beacons in the contemporary fog of pessimism and cynicism.'

Victor's story

Victor Perton became a barrister at a young age and then went into state politics. Eighteen years on, politics was changing – Victor found his work was becoming increasingly negative and he wasn't feeling fulfilled. He retired from parliament at the next election and started his own regulatory affairs business. When the government asked him to go to the US to be Trade and Investment Commissioner to the Americas, he arrived in the midst of the global financial crisis (GFC). Victor embraced the opportunity and the experience was constructive, powered by the positive stereotype Americans have of Australians. When the opportunity arose to be a senior adviser for Australia's G20 presidency, Victor was exposed to learnings and amazing people at the global super-elite level.

When Victor returned to Melbourne in 2015, he was astonished by the negativity within Australia generally, and especially towards leadership. Instead of complaining about the complainers, Victor set up the Australian Leadership Project, which interviewed more than 2500 people. The survey looked at what distinguishes Australian leaders from foreign leaders.

The survey findings revealed three key traits of Australian leaders:

1. **Egalitarian:** In Australia we demand that our leaders be egalitarian, meaning they work to ensure all people have equal rights and opportunities. The prime minister travels in the front seat of the car and we often talk to the cleaner more politely than we speak to the chairman.

2. **Self-effacing humour:** As leaders, we are confident in our ability to exert control over our own motivation, behaviour and social environment. We laugh at ourselves but take our work seriously. Many countries see self-effacing humour as a weakness, but here in Australia we see it as a statement of self-confidence.

3. **No-bullshit plain speaking:** We say what we mean and mean what we say and don't back down in what we believe in.

Victor believed that if these three qualities stood out to the interviewees, he would see many examples of Australian leaders championing those traits. He was perplexed by the reality he saw: leaders fuelled by negativity, lack of gratitude and limited understanding. It seemed that Australian leaders did not know how good they had it.

The Eureka moment

In 2017, Victor spoke at the Global Integrity Summit about the case for optimism. After three days of speeches reeking with misery, he lifted the room with his message of optimism.

Helen Clarke, head of the United Nations Development Programme and former prime minister of New Zealand, told Victor he needed to share his message by authoring a book. Victor wrote that book and Helen endorsed it.

In August 2019, Victor was asked to do some work on innovation and questioned on why he wasn't extending his work globally. Victor knew the idea had huge potential, and the Centre for Optimism was born. As I write this, the centre has attracted more than 2500 members across 52 countries after only six months of operation.

This is the question that changed it all:

What makes you optimistic?

Victor has asked this question to presidents, ministers, even women digging ditches in the back roads of India, and 99% of them said they felt lifted just by being asked the question. He has asked prisoners, murderers and drug traffickers, and shared the responses to this question. The question is now fundamental to the purpose of the Centre for Optimism.

The question can also be adapted to suit different contexts. Victor has done work with the International Congress for Tropical Medicine and Malaria and reframed the question to, 'What makes you optimistic about the eradication of malaria?'

Victor and his team want to foster infectiously optimistic leaders, and hope that those who are exposed to this question will ask it of others.

As you read this, I invite you to reflect on this question – the response could enable you to open your Gift of Optimism and how and what you have learnt from it in your life:

What makes you optimistic now, in the past, for the future?

What is optimism?

The word 'optimism' comes from the Latin *optimus,* meaning 'best'. Optimism is an internal decision framework based on inner values, goals, willingness, hope and belief.

Victor believes, as do I, that the difference between optimism and positive thinking is that the positive thinker sees good in everything, while the optimist sees the good in the now and also in the future. Positivity, I believe, is more about the present whereas optimism is about hope for now and the future – that everything will work out in the end. Victor explained that there are dark clouds that do not always have good in them, and we don't always have to believe there is a silver lining.

Optimism and gratitude underpin resilience, and gratitude is also a product of optimism. Sometimes just believing that what you have is good enough can increase optimism, even when you are struggling. It can help to compare our situation with those who may be worse off.

Pessimists versus optimists

You can't be resilient unless you are being optimistic. If you are a pessimist, there is nothing to underpin your resilience. Victor believes that limiting our consumption of negativity can help us to fuel our optimism. We can't always avoid pessimistic people and situations, but we should limit our exposure to them when we can. When around pessimism, remain as your optimistic self but slightly adapt the level of your optimism – this can create better connection and rapport.

A meditation teacher once said to Victor, 'You can mediate as much as you like but if you're sitting in a toxic swamp you will absorb some of the poison.'

Lynn Wood, founder of global idea-sharing platform IdeaSpies, believes we should all go on a 'news diet'. On the news in Australia or, indeed, most of the world, nothing good occurs. Immersing ourselves too much in this content can stifle optimism. I believe we need to be mindful as to what we give attention to – we absorb what we surround ourselves with, be it news, negative situations or people. I personally rarely watch the news and instead opt to do something that moves me or others forward.

Change your language

Critical thinking has been elevated to an almost priestly level in Australia. It is rare not to have people in meetings and boardroom sessions leaning forward and saying the word 'but'. Victor believes we need to get the people around a table to say 'and' instead – this can reduce some of the negativity and promote forward thinking in the conversation.

Reframing certain words can be powerful and bring in optimism. When researching motivational intelligence, I found that people who are highly analytical and motivated by solving problems may come across as negative. On the flip side, goal-oriented people can come across as overly optimistic. There is no right or wrong; we need to appreciate and leverage each other's differences, but not at the price of changing who we are.

Research from the University of Michigan shows that if you are married to an optimist, you may get some of the same health benefits as if you were optimistic yourself.

Why can optimism be challenging?

Victor believes many people who are optimistic can be attacked for being a Pollyanna or for being too positive. I know from experience, being an eternal optimist, that those who tend to look at the glass as half empty can find me unrealistic or just can't understand how I can stay so positive. I dial my optimism down a fraction to adapt to these people, but I never lose who I am or what I stand for.

> *Whether you think you can, or you think you can't – you're right.* —Henry Ford

Some other key challenges Victor identified include:

- **Media:** The media is so negative that even positive messages are expressed in the negative. Watching the news does nothing to foster optimism – quite the opposite.
- **Negative school curriculum:** As I write this, Victor's daughter is studying the topic of dystopia at school. Why can't utopia be studied instead?
- **Depression:** In Australia, it's estimated that 45% of people will experience a mental health condition in their lifetime.
- **People don't talk about optimism:** Rarely do people talk about optimism and what makes them optimistic. Instead, many people ask, 'What's keeping you awake at night?' We need to focus on bringing the topic of optimism into conversations and discussions, both in and out of the workplace.

Optimism in leadership

Robert Iger, Executive Chairman of the Walt Disney Company, says that one of his 10 leadership tips is to be infectiously optimistic.

> *Leaders need to be infected with optimism to lead, yet they also need to be grounded in reality.*

Research by Korn Ferry says infectious optimism is one of the three core competencies, yet people are not interviewed on this. Many are interviewed about innovation and science, but we can't be innovative without being optimistic.

The key reason Victor started the Centre for Optimism was to provide tools for leaders to be optimistic that they can also share and use within their teams.

Victor says we need to adopt habits around being optimistic. These could include things such as smiling and laughing like an optimist and reframing the way in which we greet others. I love his exercise 'my best self' where you take 15 minutes to self-reflect and ponder the question, 'What will I look like, feel like and be like in five years' time?'

> *Be a beacon of optimism in the fog of pessimism.*
> —Victor Perton

Victor's insights and the compelling reason for optimism resonated with me and reinforced that the Gift of Optimism is within us all – we just need to access it, live it and share it.

Theories on optimism

Two well-researched theories on optimism are dispositional optimism and explanatory optimism.

Charles Carver and Michael Scheier introduced the term 'dispositional optimism'. They argued that the presence of positive traits increases the chances of something good happening to us. The dispositional theory of optimism suggests that optimism leads to positive consequences in life, and pessimism leads to stressful outcomes and increased dissatisfaction.

Martin Seligman derived the explanatory model of optimism from his concept of 'learned helplessness'. This approach explained optimism as the way people perceive and interpret events, more than their in-built personal traits.

I believe both theories depend upon the person and context. My family – especially my husband Brett, stepdad Kym and brother Dean – have an innate ability, no matter how challenging things are, to tap into their positive traits to get through. They tend to focus on what they do have, accept that the past can't be changed and remind themselves that what they have been through before they can get through again. Kym always reminds me that there are people worse off – he remembers witnessing much poverty when working in developing countries in his 45-year career with Mitsubishi Motors. I have found that certain people are naturally more optimistic than others, but I have also worked with people who are pessimistic and choose to work on their optimism and improve it.

The impact of optimism on health and wellbeing

I know that when I am happy and optimistic, I feel fulfilled and motivated and this results in me being physically, mentally and emotionally healthy. On the flip side, at times when I have had to suppress emotions or my opinion, or have been surrounded by toxic situations or people, the opposite has occurred.

Dr Eric Kim, visiting scientist at Harvard University, believes that optimism could be linked to better health and mortality for several reasons. Optimistic people often have healthier eating, exercise and smoking habits. Optimism may somehow impact biological function, potentially through lower levels of inflammation or better immune function. Optimistic people may also have better coping skills, as optimism builds resilience.

A meta-analysis published in JAMA Network Open looked at 15 studies that measured optimism and pessimism. Researchers from 10 of the studies, which included data on more than 209,000 people, found that compared with pessimists, optimists had a 35% lower risk for heart-related events.

Studies on the effect of optimism on victims of natural disasters found that people who received positive interventions could cope better with their situation.

An Austrian study showed that optimists are less likely to suffer from chronic insomnia. It was also shown that more sleep improves your optimism and that this can help people increase their dispositional optimism.

If the positive impact on our health and wellbeing isn't compelling enough, I don't know what is. The Gift of Optimism is there for all of us to unwrap – we just need to untie the bow, open the wrapping and look at what is accessible to all of us.

The four stages to optimism

Living a life filled with optimism is an ongoing journey. The beliefs, traits and behaviours we build upon can assist us in reflecting on the positive aspects of our lives, fuelling us forward.

I know from experience that self-belief, and belief and hope in others and situations, is foundational to building optimism. If you add to that a healthy dose of gratitude and positivity, you give yourself the best chance to move from pessimism to optimism.

The Gift of Optimism

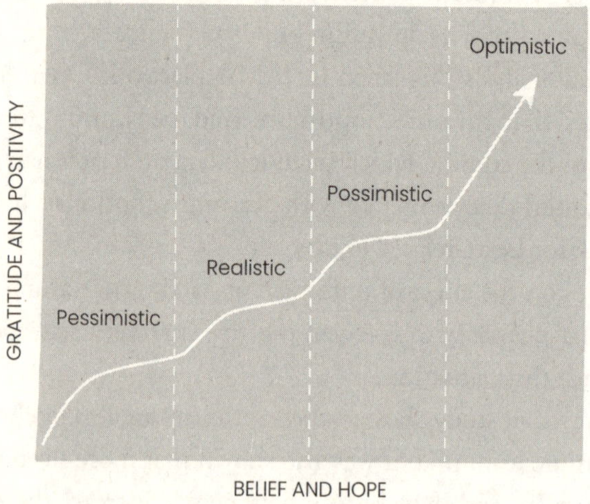

Let's take a closer look at the four stages to optimism.

Stage 1 – Pessimistic

If you're in this stage, belief, hope, gratitude and positivity are non-existent, or you are unaware of how you feel about optimism and pessimism. Maybe past events, people and situations have led you to feel that the glass is always half empty. You are looking at what could go wrong instead of what could go right. You may not be aware of the effect this has on you and others. At this stage the Gift of Optimism is tightly wrapped up.

Stage 2 – Realistic

You are looking at what could be and weighing up thoughts, feelings and actions. You may be starting to build belief in self, others and situations you are facing. There may be a glimmer of hope that things could be good and you may start to open the door to invite gratitude and positive thinking into your life. You are untying the bow on the Gift of Optimism.

Stage 3 – Possimistic™

This stage is what I call 'possimistic'. You see the possibilities and know that optimism can fuel them. You are unwrapping what could be. Your belief and hope are high, and you are practising the habits of gratitude and positive inner dialogue. You feel hope for the future and are positive in what could be. You are highly aware of the power of optimism and possibility.

Stage 4 – Optimistic

If you are at this stage, well done! You have unwrapped the Gift of Optimism. You live with high belief and hope and practise gratitude and positivity to deal with whatever you are being faced with, day to day. Continuing these practices and behaviours will ensure you are brimming with optimism and sharing this with people you surround yourself with, in and out of the workplace.

Wherever you currently sit on the pathway to optimism can change depending on the context of the situation. It is up to you to step into your power to move towards optimism and embed the tips and tools within this chapter that resonate with you.

> *Life is like a mirror. Smile at it and it smiles back at you.*
> —Peace Pilgrim

The six keys to optimism

We will now unpack the keys to build optimism in your life and develop it so that you can lead with strength, overcome adversity and keep moving forward.

1. Make your self-talk optimistic

Our thoughts create our feelings and attitude, which results in our actions. Eliminating limiting beliefs can increase optimism, along with reframing our inner dialogue. Simply flipping a thought such as 'This is a horrible situation' to 'What can I do to make the most of this situation?' can change the way you look at the world and increase the hope you have to move through it. Flip the script to serve you and how you feel. Remind yourself of the times you have been optimistic and conquered challenges.

2. Remember to smile

Make eye contact and smile, even to strangers – it's more than likely they will smile back. Who doesn't love it when someone smiles at them? I know I do!

Smiling activates the release of endorphins, dopamine and serotonin into your bloodstream – feel-good messengers known to work towards fighting stress. This helps your body relax and can lower blood pressure and heart rate.

3. Greet with intention

Instead of using the everyday, mundane 'How are you going?', ask 'What is the best thing that has happened to you today?' My mum asked my sister and me this every day growing up, and this question serves me even now. Share something interesting when you start a conversation: it could be a compliment, a good-news story or a question filled with curiosity. There is good in most things if you are present to unwrapping the gift of the situation.

4. Get laughing

Laughter can bring people together and establish amazing connections. Remember those times you laughed so hard because those around you were laughing? Laughing stimulates the motor region of the brain to become active, and that's what produces the physical reaction of laughing and the vocal expulsion of sound. It is known that when we laugh it can boost heart rate and mood, as well as the production of certain antibodies, strengthening our immune system.

5. Surround yourself with optimists

There is a saying that goes, 'We are the sum of the people we spend the most time with'. We need to be aware of who we interact with and limit exposure to pessimistic people and situations, which can become like optimism vampires – draining our energy, headspace and ultimately our optimism reserves. Ensure you spend time with people who light you up. When going through challenges I ensure I tap into others who energise me and for whom I can do the same.

6. Be grateful

Fostering an attitude of gratitude can maximise optimism in multiple ways. It helps us reframe memories of unpleasant events in a way that decreases their negative emotional impact. We can let challenges deepen the way in which we are grateful – they can show us not to take things for granted. Practise gratitude in a way that works for you; it could be as simple as diarising thoughts, sending a thankyou note or simply thanking someone verbally. Being grateful helps us focus on the things we do have and the possibility those things bring.

Now it's time to unwrap your GIFT of Optimism

Take some time to think about the questions below.

G Grow

- What key lessons has the gift taught you?
- In what ways has it helped you to learn and grow?

I Integrate

- How will you incorporate these lessons into your life moving forward?
- What do you need to be aware of and what could get in the way of you actioning these lessons?

F Facilitate

- What lessons from this gift can you share with others professionally or personally?
- Who will you share these with and how will you share this gift?

T Transform

- How will you know that this gift has transformed you and others?
- When will you share this gift with others?

The Optimism Bomboniera

- Optimism – the belief that good things will happen and that things work out in the end – is an internal decision framework based on values, goals, willingness, hope and belief.
- Reflect and answer regularly, 'What makes you optimistic?' Ask others and share your responses, in and out of work.
- Mental, physical and emotional health can be improved by adopting an optimistic mindset, its habits and behaviours. Optimism's multifaceted benefits can flow on.
- Optimism is contagious and a trait of most successful leaders. Bringing optimism into your life will positively affect you and your teams; consider the cost of *not* bringing it in.
- Practise gratitude and foster hope and belief to open your Gift of Optimism. Greet people with intention, focus on what's possible and good, smile, laugh and limit your exposure to pessimism.

Eight

THE GIFT OF COURAGE

> *Courage is resistance to fear, mastery of fear – not absence of fear.* —Mark Twain

In this chapter, we will unwrap the Gift of Courage. We will look at what it takes for us, as human beings, to tap into our inner strength and access all we have within us to live and lead with courage and share this with others.

We will unwrap:

- six keys to courage
- three key operating zones we can access courage from
- the GIFT process to help you unwrap your Gift of Courage and share it.

But first, I'd like to share one of the greatest stories of courage I ever learned – from my own family. I was given access to this story only recently and it is special to be able to share it with you.

The Giarrussos' story

This story takes you back to 1943, when a family took one of the biggest risks – to start a new life on the other side of the world.

My nonno, Paul, owned a leather shop in Catania, Sicily. (I blame this for my innate addiction to shoes.) He tanned leather and suede to supply to shoe and coat manufacturers. The entire family lived above the shop in a *palazzo*, with a lavish marble staircase at the main entrance.

Life was good while prime minister Benito Mussolini was in power, giving holidays to the poor and assisting new mothers with money and goods. However, he didn't support bad news in newspapers and only those who had identification to prove they were a member of the Fascist Party were allowed to travel or work.

Many people remember Mussolini as a good leader – until he teamed up with Hitler.

Although the Italians and the Germans were allies in World War II, the Sicilians resented the Germans taking over their towns. Many aggressive soldiers abused the local people, ordering them out of shops while demanding the best of everything. My nonna felt uneasy. The young women were frightened. My Aunty Mary still recalls the eerie sound of the soldiers' boots as they marched along the cobbled village roads.

Everything changed

At dawn on 10 July 1943, when the Americans invaded Sicily, everything changed. Operation Husky involved 150,000 troops. Air and sea landings using 3000 ships and 4000 aircraft were directed at the southern shores of the island.

Before long, warning sirens alerted everyone to shelter in their basements. Up to five families would huddle in this dark, damp space; some nights, six alerts were signalled. Many nearby buildings were bombed.

A beautiful, tranquil southern Italian island was now at the centre of a war. Living on meagre food coupons was hard, with little access to things such as coffee and sugar and other staples that we take for granted these days. My grandparents struggled to keep their business going with three children to keep safe. The food coupons ran out; luckily the family was seen as wealthy, so they never went too long without anything. Nonno was able to access goods via the black market, but many others were not so fortunate. My generous grandparents often had people over and fed them; workers from their business stayed and refuelled over a meal with them.

The only distraction to pass the time was to listen to the radio or play records. When they could, the family went away on weekends to their property in Misterbianco, 30 minutes away – a brief escape from the nightmare that was unfolding at home.

The bombings

As the war continued, Dad's family relocated to the neighbouring village of Vizzini. At the peak of the bombing, they retreated to caves just out of town for three to four days at a time. It was more crowded than the *palazzo* basement and even the sheep would join them in there. When they returned to Catania, they found bomb fragments that had come through the roof and landed on my grandparents' bed. Even during this time, the Americans were more like friends than enemies, frequently giving the children chocolates and biscuits.

My father, Tony Giarrusso, was born in 1946. He grew up with two older brothers and a sister, Mary; 16 years older, she was like a second mother to him. She had attended primary school until grade 4, when her mother became ill and she had to leave to look after her father and then-two brothers. The family was well enough off to have a maid; despite this, Aunty Mary was still expected to assist with household duties.

Tony wasn't yet born when Aunty Mary and Nonna were visiting a shop and a fortune teller asked to read Nonna's palm. She predicted three things: something valuable would be lost, the family would go abroad and Mary would marry a foreigner. Little did Mary know that all three predictions would come true.

Leaving everything

After the war, my nonno's business started to suffer the effects of cheap imports. A proud man, he could not face working for somebody else. So the Giarrussos decided to leave everything and travel to America or Australia. Nonno's sister had already moved to America with her husband to bring the family over. But Nonna's brother Chico persuaded them to come to Australia instead and stay with him. Mary was 19 and Dad was three years old.

No-one in the family could speak any language but Italian. Nonno said they would go for three to four years, long enough to get back on their feet, and then return to Italy.

They purchased tickets for the trip by selling their house, their shop, the property and all their possessions.

In 1949 the family left Italy aboard Greek cargo ship *Cyrenia,* used to transport people leaving Germany. Nonno, Nonna and their four children, aged from three to 19, sailed for Australia crammed into one small cabin with a bunk bed, their lives contained in a suitcase each and one large trunk.

Aunty Mary remembers there being a lot of Polish and Jewish people on board, many with numbers tattooed on their wrists – a blunt reminder of the war. There were no other Italians on the ship, and all the music and food was Greek.

Most of the family suffered seasickness throughout the trip. My dad developed measles and was quarantined from the rest of the family.

The trip that changed the family's lives lasted 29 days.

Making a new home

When Dad and family arrived at the station pier in Australia, their uncle was there to greet them and take them all to his farm in Koo Wee Rup, where they lived in a wooden house. Aunty Mary worried it would burn down – there were no wooden houses in Sicily.

There was no work in the country, so my aunty was sent to live with an Italian family in Melbourne, and worked as a seamstress in a clothing factory.

The family ended up residing in a small street in North Melbourne, in a two-bedroom place with no bathroom – they had to go to the City Baths to bathe. It was a far cry from their life in Italy. Nonna got the family settled and Dad and his brothers went to the local Catholic school. Aunty Mary fell in love with a Cypriot man from her workplace; within a year of arriving she was married, with a baby on the way.

The decision to stay was inevitable – their life and growing family were in Australia. My grandparents moved to Essendon to be near Aunty Mary and her family. Nonno continued to work at a tannery and Nonna worked as a dressmaker until they retired.

It was 30 years before they had the opportunity to have a holiday and go back to Italy.

Courage comes from within, which is why I wanted to share this story – one that is close to my heart. It teaches us the Gift of Courage and what we, as human beings, are capable of.

My grandparents were young, they had never been outside Italy, yet they had the confidence to fuel their courage to up and leave with the hope of a better life. I find it hard to comprehend the dread my grandmother must have felt and the courage she had to find to stay strong and positive to support and protect her family.

This was definitely a Pass the Parcel gift, meaning it was a challenging situation that was unexpected in their lifetime. On the Gift Timeline we went through earlier, this is a hidden gift.

I get goosebumps thinking of the uncertainty they must have felt, not knowing what could happen at any time. As I write this, we are facing the COVID-19 pandemic. Across the world people are dying, businesses are being shut down or heavily affected and our state has gone into lockdown for a second time. Uncertainty, anxiety and an eerie quietness are in the air. We rely on technology to bridge the gap of connection with family, friends, work colleagues and clients. In supporting others through this time, I have had to dig deep within to feel, think and act with courage and focus on what can be done and how to be of service to those around me. We all have the courage and grit within us to access when faced with adversity.

To me, this is our version of what my grandparents went through. This is our war, in our lifetime.

It is so important to unwrap the gifts we face before they are lost forever and the lessons never discussed, let alone applied, to help and inspire others.

Thinking of my grandparents and what they achieved reminds me that the Gift of Courage is within all of us. We just need to unwrap it.

How different things would be right now if they had stayed in Italy. I wouldn't be here and you wouldn't be reading this book. Every decision you've made affects what you are doing today: small ripples can create waves.

I would do anything to ask them how they 'did' courage, but many on that side of my family are no longer with us. I know that what they experienced set them up for what was to come during their life in Australia, such as losing my dad and his brother, both under 51 years old.

Courage builds courage and layers upon itself over time.

I believe courage transforms fear, and sometimes even shame, into determination.

At times when we want to give in, courage helps us continue; it's the fuel to propel us forward. It helps us reach beyond our comfort zone and welcome new challenges. Above all, it helps us to accept the challenges life throws at us.

The six keys to courage

Courage is made up of some key ingredients. As with any recipe, all these ingredients need to be incorporated in the right amounts for the perfect dish. Let's take a look at the six keys to courage.

1. Have purpose

Having a deep intention of what you want can fuel your inner courage.

Purpose is linked to your outcome, where you are heading, why you are doing what you do and where you are directing your energy. Don't make the mistake of getting attached to your outcome; be open to change, if needed. A well-achieved purpose has to be *on purpose* or there is no point. Purpose comes from the heart; purpose has to be felt, not just thought, especially when facing something that requires copious amounts of courage. Having a strong, aligned purpose allows motivation to take hold.

The purpose of my family moving from Italy to Australia was to start a new life in a country where they could rebuild their wealth, be safe and have a good quality of life for their children – a clear, strong purpose with intent.

2. Have awareness

As outlined earlier, awareness is the foundation of the Gift Mindset. It is also a key component of courage. To make any change or face any challenge you need to be aware of yourself, your strengths and your weaknesses. You need to be in touch with how you feel internally by tuning into logic, as well as your heart and your intuition – what many call their 'gut feeling'. Your gut contains a network of over 100 million neurons – as many as a cat's brain. Countless feelings and thoughts start from here.

When my grandparents moved to Australia, they would have had to be aware of what Australia was like, where they were going to reside and the financial support they needed to do it. All these factors that allowed them to use their courage and make the move had to be in their awareness. I believe their thoughts, feelings and feedback from around them fuelled their decision and courage.

3. Believe in yourself

A newspaper editor once fired Walt Disney because 'he lacked imagination and had no good ideas'. After numerous bankruptcies he went on to build the first-ever Disneyland, even after the first park in Anaheim was rejected.

Van Gogh only ever officially sold one painting in his lifetime, and that was to a sister of one his friends for a measly $50 in today's currency. He still went on to paint more than 800 masterpieces.

What if Disney and Van Gogh had given up? What would we be missing out on today? Mickey Mouse and the characters of *Fantasia* would not have lit up the hearts and minds of children the world over. Van Gogh's world-famous paintings and influence within the 20th-century art movement would be missing – who could estimate the impact of that on the art world today?

They both had a strong belief in themselves and their ideas and dreams. They were tenacious and had a clear purpose to which they were fearlessly committed.

Successful people have a strong commitment to action; they don't need to question what they believe to be true. Beliefs are things we consider to be true. They form the basis of our thoughts and influence the choices we make. To be courageous we need high levels of self-belief in our abilities, skills and what we can achieve.

4. Live your values

Identifying our values can be a great conduit to understanding our boundaries. Simply put, values are things that are important to us. We all have values that determine our everyday decisions, from where we bank to what car we drive and who we allow into our inner circle. Values are the underlying linchpin to every decision we make, both personally and professionally. We aren't usually consciously aware of these, despite the fact that they drive our decisions and our life choices. Values change, and by being aware of what they are we can gain a better understanding of why we feel how we feel when our values are challenged, and when we are living in alignment with them.

My grandparents knew their values; I imagine they would have included security, safety, family and community, and freedom. These would have aligned with the reason to move and therefore contributed to the courage they displayed.

5. Be open to failure

Vulnerability is the new black and I can't agree more that we need to be open and vulnerable to be courageous. We need to put ourselves out there, take risks, embrace uncertainty and be open for what comes to us, as my grandparents did. They had no idea what would happen on that voyage, let alone what would await them in Australia. We all have what I call a risk barometer, and I believe that moving across the world rates pretty highly when it comes to risky decisions.

In the workplace we need to be just as courageous as we are in our personal lives. If not, innovation, creativity, transformation and the future of work are doomed. We need to take risks, embrace the unknown and back ourselves, and remember if we do fail we can only learn from the experience.

In Brené Brown's documentary *The Call to Courage*, she talks about stepping out into the metaphorical 'arena' and backing yourself. This really resonated with me:

> *I'm going to live in the arena. I'm going to be brave with my life. I'm going to show up. I'm going to take chances, and if you're brave with your life, if you choose to live in the arena, you're going to get your ass kicked. You're going to fall, you're going to fail, you're going to know heartbreak. Today, I choose courage over comfort.*

6. Trust

To be courageous we need to trust ourselves and those involved in what we are setting out to do. My nonna obviously trusted my nonno, to move to the other side of the world with four children and little money. She would have had to have the courage to trust and the trust to stay courageous.

To trust is to have a confident reliance on the character, ability, strength, or truth of someone or something you are pursuing. We also need to trust ourselves and this comes from believing in our abilities and the 'why' of what we are doing. To stay strong and be brave and fearless, we need to remind ourselves of times we have trusted before and anchor the positive outcomes and experiences we have gleaned. Anything we have faced before, we can face again. It becomes part of who we are.

As you can see, these six keys to courage intertwine. You can't have high self-belief if you aren't trusting and your purpose can only be as strong as the alignment of your values. By reflecting on these six elements you can enhance your Gift of Courage.

Three key zones

Courage has a lot to do with getting out of our comfort zone or 'safe zone' and moving into our 'stretch zone'.

In a safe zone there is no growth – nothing changes and there is very little challenge.

I believe there are three key zones we can choose to operate from:

1. **Safe zone:**
   - Stay comfortable with little stress
   - Find excuses
   - Live life on autopilot
   - Lack confidence
2. **Step-up zone:**
   - Embrace change and new things
   - Acquire new skills

- Expand oneself
- Face change and challenges

3. **Stretch zone:**
   - Pursue dreams
   - Set BHAG (big hairy audacious goals that scare you)
   - Find true purpose
   - Get comfortable being uncomfortable

To break out of the safe zone, stop focusing on what you need to do; your purpose will guide you. Instead, be still and think about who you need to be. It's not always about the process, but who you're becoming to make it happen.

We have all heard that person say, 'When I have the money, I'll buy a big house and have a holiday and then I'll change jobs and be happy.' This is wrong on so many levels. It's great to start with the end in mind, but who do you need to be, day in and day out, to fuel your actions to achieve your plans? It is vital to reflect on who you need to be right now. It will help you break out of your comfort zone.

Jayden's story

My client Jayden was a senior leader who was extremely busy working *in* his team, not *on* it. Working day and night, he was burnt out with no time to create or lead strategic vision for his team or organisation. This was affecting his health and emotional wellbeing. He missed some of his mentoring sessions with me – a sign that something needed to change.

A lightbulb moment occurred when we worked through where he was at and discovered, together, that he was using procrastination as a strategy. By keeping busy, he had no time to stop and be who he needed to be. Instead, he was doing the wrong things at the wrong time and, therefore, the results weren't anywhere near where they needed to be. There was no change, innovation or risk being taken within his team and this was impacting the sustainability of the business.

Jayden was clearly in a safe zone; his behaviour kept him in a place that was safe and easy and, like an express train, he made no time to stop and get off to see what was going on. He wasn't aware of the values or beliefs that were driving him. Delving into this and working through what he valued and who he needed to be resulted in some profound insights. He needed to be present, strategic, future-focused and courageous – words that changed his beliefs around what he needed to do. Yes, he had to bust out of his safe zone, but the payoff was huge.

As a leader, failing to show courage can contribute to a 'safe' culture where uncertainty isn't embraced and long-term creativity, innovation and change are stifled. How you display courage and own it can have a cascade effect. Courage is a good thing: when we do things that frighten us or get us out of our comfort zone we are growing, and in the process growing others.

My question to you

What will it cost you, your team and your organisation if you do not break through your safe zone and have the courage to act and be bold?

Do keep in mind that courage can be hidden; it's not always a roar. For example, getting up in front of a group to present publicly can look easy and not necessarily be seen as a courageous act to others. For the person experiencing it, though, it takes a lot of courage.

> *Integrity is choosing courage over comfort; it's choosing what is right over what's fun, fast or easy; and it's practicing your values not just protecting them.* —Brené Brown

Now it's time to unwrap your GIFT of Courage

Take some time to think about the questions below.

G Grow

- What key lessons has the gift taught you?
- In what ways has it helped you to learn and grow?

I Integrate

- How will you incorporate these lessons into your life moving forward?
- What do you need to be aware of and what could get in the way of you actioning these lessons?

F Facilitate

- What lessons from this gift can you share with others professionally or personally?
- Who will you share these with and how will you share this gift?

T Transform

- How will you know that this gift has transformed you and others?
- When will you share this gift with others?

Your Courage Bomboniera

- Courage can be hidden; it doesn't always come in the form of something significant and noticeable. A small thing you do or approach differently can result in a ripple that may create a wave of change.
- Tap into the six keys that drive courage: purpose, awareness, belief, aligned values, vulnerability and trust.
- Get comfortable being uncomfortable: take yourself from the 'safe zone' to the 'stretch zone'.
- Change and innovation comes from being courageous. Choose to live 'in the arena' and be brave with your life.
- Share your Gift of Courage. Doing this will reinforce the qualities, skills and traits that will allow you to build on this and assist others in the process.

Nine

THE GIFT OF RESILIENCE

You may encounter many defeats, but you must not be defeated. In fact, it may be necessary to encounter the defeats, so you can know who you are, what you can rise from, how you can still come out of it. —Maya Angelou

In this chapter, we will unwrap the Gift of Resilience and the skills and traits that make up living and developing it. Building resilience is a layered process where we stack experiences, learnings and new ways of thinking. It deserves to be understood and shared.

We will unwrap:

- the three elements essential to resilience
- the six keys to resilience
- the GIFT process to unwrap your Gift of Resilience and share it.

But first, I'd like to share a client's story with you. In both our personal and professional lives, we all face many situations and people that require us to tap into our resilience. Steven, a client of mine, shares his story that I believe you will all relate to in some way. Your story may be slightly different, but I'm sure the way in which he has dealt with a challenge will resonate with you.

Steven's story

Steven Pereira is Chief Information Officer at GS1 Australia.

'Nothing is guaranteed,' he says. 'Even if you have been in employment with the same company for over 17 years, there are no guarantees that they will treat you any better than if you had been with the company for 17 months.

'I was with a major Australian corporation for 17 years and had accrued a long history of delivering major initiatives, both in Western Australia and at the corporation's Melbourne head office. Over that time, I held a variety of roles, from operational to corporate engineering, from IT to project management, and from ecommerce to finance – the latter was the most closely related to my commerce degree from the University of Western Australia.'

Everything changed

'One morning in 1995 I was called into my manager's office and out of the blue he mentioned that I was doing a good job. This did not surprise me, because I knew that I had been (said humbly). In fact, the principle I have always worked to was inherited from my late father, who taught me, "Do not work for mere pay but from a real desire to serve. Do not look down on the people given into your care, but be an example."

'Later that day I was called into the same office, this time with my manager's manager, and was told that I was being reassigned to other duties. The new role would be called "Special Projects". The term had then, and perhaps still has, a not-so-endearing connotation.

'I was devasted. I fell into the typical grief cycle of shock – anger – telling my story – helplessness – acceptance – moving on.

Yet it is fair to say that I did not remain in the depression or helplessness cycle long enough for it to entrap me, because of the faith and belief system I held at that time.'

Acceptance is key

'I accepted the change because previous years had shown that restructures in this organisation occurred with such regularity – every six months – that such a change would not likely be a permanent one.

'Some folks who are faced with a similar situation become so embittered that it begins to eat them from the inside out, figuratively speaking. I know of one example where the person who met a similar fate was so angry and bitter that they refused to enter the company's stores and shop there. For all I know, that bitterness is still being harboured more than two decades on.

'I continued to work as I did before and when I resigned from the company many colleagues and managers from various parts of the organisation gathered at my farewell reception. I still have the card where all of them signed their names and wrote a comment. From time to time I do reflect on the card and read the comments in it. It serves as a reminder of the legacy I left behind.'

What it taught me

'It is not what you do that matters, it is the impact that your work has on people's lives and the human connections you make that really matter.

'As it turned out, a few months after my fork-in-the-road experience I was invited to apply for a job in a new organisation. I believe my faith played a big part in my journey in all aspects of my life. I believe it was by divine appointment that I have been employed by this new company for more than 24 years now, rising to senior ranks across various departments. I am still enjoying what I do, still adding value to the company and being a positive example to all those in my sphere of influence.

'This experience taught me the gift of resilience. What served me well was adopting a positive attitude and having a belief system that was able to sustain, empower and propel me forward in the face of any adversity.'

The word 'resilience' comes from the Latin word *resilire*, which means to leap back, recoil or rebound. It is the strength of spirit to deal with and recover from adversity.

In the social, behavioural and biological sciences, 'resilience' is used in a variety of ways and contexts – sometimes as an individual characteristic, sometimes as a process and sometimes as an outcome. It is shaped by the accumulation of experiences – both positive and negative – and the continuing development of adaptive coping skills that are attuned to those experiences.

Steven's story would be familiar to many of you. It can be much easier to take the path of feeling bitter and backing this up with disempowering behaviour than, as he did, owning the situation, staying true to your values and beliefs and using this to fuel resilience to serve you for the better.

Steven chose his thoughts and, therefore, what he felt and how he responded to the situation. He was highly aware and accepting of the situation. I know firsthand that he still shares his lessons and learnings to grow future leaders across GS1 Australia; I've invited Steven to speak and share his wisdom at workshop events I have run outside of GS1.

The gift of courage connects strongly to resilience, along with hope, and this can assist us when facing loss, tragedy or disappointment, as well as fuel us on our journey of success. It can help us engage in life fully and stay strong, with the flexibility to bounce back. Hardship can cultivate your character and, as we know, your reputation is only a shadow of this. Your character is made up of all you have been through and overcome.

Look at resilience as a collection of skills that we can call upon when facing adversity. And, like any muscle, resilience can be built up.

Experience builds resilience

Resilience results from a dynamic interaction between internal qualities and external experiences.

I believe that the more you go through, both personally and professionally, the stronger you get. Each experience deepens your ability to see the challenging times and people in your life as gifts, and to identify and apply the lessons learnt from these to propel you forward.

Thomas Edison created thousands of prototypes of the incandescent lightbulb before he mastered it. He was awarded more than 1000 patents before getting it right and could easily have given up. All the tens of thousands of failures during his working life simply showed him how *not* to invent something. The most amazing inventions of the early 20th century – including the telegraph, phonograph and motion picture – came from his unstoppable resilience. He could have let failure derail him, but instead he demonstrated resilience at the highest level in order to overcome his challenges. Imagine if he had given up? The world could be a very different place now.

> *I have not failed. I have just found 10,000 ways that won't work.* —Thomas Edison

In a nutshell, resilience is the strength of spirit to recover from adversity. It enables us to find hope and the courage to continue, even when faced with tragedy or negative circumstances. Resilience isn't a trait but, instead, a result of tapping into internal and external resources.

Three elements essential to resilience

Research published in the *Journal of Humanistic Psychology* showed that there are three elements essential to resilience:

1. **Challenge rather than crisis:** Resilient people look at mistakes and failures as lessons. They tend to reframe a paralysing event as a challenge. *This in itself can change your mindset to be even more resilient.*
2. **Commitment to goals:** Resilient people are committed in work, relationships, friendships, beliefs and things that they care about. *Being committed will give you a compelling reason to get out of bed in the morning.*
3. **Personal control:** Resilient people focus their energy and time, putting their efforts where they can have the most impact, and where they feel empowered and confident. *Focusing on what we can influence allows us to stop worrying about events that are out of our control, which can make us feel lost and powerless.*

The six keys to resilience

We will now examine the skills needed to build resilience and how to develop them so we can lead with strength to overcome adversity and keep moving forward.

1. Develop supportive relationships

Strong, supportive relationships are vital to building resilience. As human beings we are wired to connect. Strong connections at work make us happier in our roles and more resistant to stress. Strong friendships in our personal life make us more resilient as we have a strong network to fall back on.

Social support gives us access to practical support, emotional support, support with decision-making – all of this helps us in facing challenges. Many researchers suggest that living a more altruistic life where we give selflessly to others helps us be more resilient.

Replacing face-to-face contact with family and friends with messages on social media, emails or text messages could double our risk of depression. People in contact with family and friends at least three times a week have been found to have the lowest level of depressive symptoms. Harvard University states:

> *The single most common factor for children who develop resilience is at least one stable and committed relationship with a supportive parent, caregiver, or other adult. These relationships provide the personalized responsiveness, scaffolding, and protection that buffer children from developmental disruption.*

My questions to you

- Who is in your support network?
- What part do you play for each other?
- How could you better utilise and give back to your support network?

> *How resilient we are may have as much to do with our social milieu and circle of support as it does with our personal strengths.* —Jill Suttie

2. Foster an attitude of gratitude

Research shows that taking the time to develop an attitude of gratitude can build a kind of psychological immune system, making us more resilient to stress.

Feelings, actions and our mindset flow from the way we look at the world and how we think about the situation. To change our feelings, we can start by thinking about what we are grateful for. Often, we find our feelings scary and confusing, so we keep them at a distance. However, shutting off our feelings not only backfires, but drains us of the psychological energy that is needed to build resilience. We need our feelings in order to find satisfaction, meaning and pleasure in life.

Gratitude can maximise happiness in multiple ways, and one reason is that it helps us reframe memories of unpleasant events in a way that decreases their negative emotional impact and lets in optimism. We can let challenges deepen the way in which we are grateful – they can show us not to take things for granted.

Looking back is about learning and looking forward is about progressing. Gratitude provides a perspective from which we can look at our entire life and not be overwhelmed by temporary circumstances. Emotions are hard to control – gratitude comes easily when things are going well, but it's not easy to feel grateful and happy when we're facing a crisis.

Being grateful is a choice. It is important to know the difference between being thankful and being grateful. I believe thankful is a feeling whereas grateful is an action. We express gratitude to ourselves or others.

Accessing and sustaining positive emotions is key in building resilience. Focusing our attention on how far we have come can provide positive reinforcement and fuel our thoughts to overcome challenges and setbacks. It helps us to see how far we have come and to review where we are now. It's like looking in the rear-vision mirror of a car – what you pass goes by quickly, so it's easy to miss a beautiful landmark or a life lesson that you could share.

Remembering the tough times can help us reaffirm that we got through a challenge. Keep in mind that anything you have overcome you can overcome again.

It is important to know what helped and also what hindered you, so you can be aware of what could get in the way. When I look back at losing my dad, I know that perseverance, a 'yes' mindset and a focus on giving to others helped get me through a difficult time. I put energy into a new job and tapped into thoughts of how proud my dad would have been. This assisted me to move forward.

When looking back, take what you need, leave what you don't and then move on.

My questions to you

Take the time to reflect on a past or present crisis. The goal here is not to relive the experience, but rather to get a new perspective on it.

Ask yourself:

- What did the experience teach me?
- What things or people can I be thankful for?
- What capabilities, qualities and skills have got me to where I am today?

3. Develop empathy

When someone opens up to you about feeling overstretched and tired, how do you respond? Do you respond with empathy, or do you shut off as you have your own stuff to deal with?

By tuning in and almost physically experiencing what another may be going through, you will have the closest chance of understanding the other person and experiencing true empathetic connection.

The Gift of Empathy is a standalone gift in this book, but it is also one of the key skills that make up resilience for you and for others.

We are all wired to connect, and you can forge, maintain and grow meaningful relationships simply by consciously focusing on extending empathy to yourself and others.

We can improve our communication and influence when we have empathy. 'Feeling in' to others helps us to resolve differences and manage challenging situations better. This decreases the level of stress we sometimes experience in challenging times and, in turn, can increase our resilience.

Empathy is a key asset needed in today's world to thrive, not just survive. We, as human beings, are wired to be empathetic. Practising empathy fosters curiosity about others, which can lead us to teach and, in the process, learn. The skill of empathy teaches us about ourselves in the process, thus building on resilience.

My questions to you

Reflect on a challenging time when you have shown empathy to another.

- How did you do this?
- What was the response?

4. Reframe the script

Rumination is the process of reliving an event over and over in our heads. This can cause us to rehash the pain when recalling a challenging event, and is necessary only until it no longer serves us. Reframing the experience is a great way to reflect on a challenge to help us move forward. One way this can be done is through the practice of expressive writing. Externalising our thoughts, values and beliefs can assist us in gaining new insights.

A study found that people who did expressive writing for four days were healthier six weeks later and happier up to three months later, in comparison to those who wrote about superficial topics.

By confronting and writing about ideas and events, one at a time, we can gain new perspectives, and so craft our own narrative. This process gives us a sense of control and can help us glean the lessons and the upside of the experience. Capturing three positives about the crisis or challenge can help us become more engaged and reframe our beliefs about the situation.

This needs to be a regular practice. I encourage my clients to do this whenever they are facing challenges at work or home, and to make the exercise a habit.

My exercise for you

- Write freehand for 20 minutes about a particular issue or challenge.
- Do this once a day for four consecutive days.
- Note the three positive outcomes or lessons gleaned.

> *Habits are the compound interest of self-improvement. The same way that money multiplies through compound interest, the effects of your habits multiply as you repeat them. They seem to make little difference on any given day and yet the impact they deliver over the months and years can be enormous.*
>
> —James Clear, *Atomic Habits*

5. Spark your motivation

Motivation has been researched for at least 80 years and the findings from studies by figures such as Frederick Herzberg, Abraham Maslow, John Hunt and Clayton Alderfer still resonate. However, working practices have changed and now the focus is on variables such as work–life balance, flexible working hours, working virtually (from home) and performance objectives. We now need to consider motivation as a key ingredient in building resilience both in and out of the workplace.

Your motivation is simply the thing that lights you up. Many people think of motivation as the thing they are good at doing, but it's more than that. It is that the thing you enjoy; that gives you a pep in your step.

When facing adversity, tapping into skills alone is not enough. If you can identify and focus on what engages you, this can drive you forward to keep going. Motivation, either intrinsic (internal) or extrinsic (external), overlays an energy on any skill: it's the fuel to succeed and exceed. It's the force behind us, driving what we know and learn.

Imagine you are a lighthouse. In order to project light out to sea, you need to have everything in order within the lighthouse to give you the fuel to burn your light – a bit like motivation. You could also think of the things that motivate you as your northern stars: they keep you on track and fired up to stay the course. These things could come in the form of situations, people and the things you pursue, learn and do.

What lights me up? Connection, contribution, achieving goals and getting to think outside the square. Tapping into these things in tough times can help me progress forward.

My questions to you

- What are the things and who are the people who light you up?
- How are you going to bring more of this into every day, especially when challenged?

6. Confront your fears

We all have fears we avoid facing at times. Maybe it's public speaking, deep water or heights; maybe it's voicing your opinion at a meeting. The more we avoid facing what we fear, the bigger the fear grows. In my experience, many people have never attempted the thing they most fear – no wonder the story in our minds makes the fear seem bigger than it actually is.

Years ago, when I was running a program for the long-term unemployed, someone said to me that FEAR is simply False Evidence Appearing Real. I love this! Upon reflection I realised that many fears I had were false and only existed in my head.

It's a good idea to 'rewind to remind' yourself of the things you have overcome and the skills, qualities and traits that enabled you to do so. Anything we've done we can usually do again and it's powerful to reinforce the fears and uncomfortable situations you have already worked through.

The best way I have found to confront my fears is to slowly but repeatedly expose myself to them. It's a bit like eating an elephant – only small bites are necessary, and then you can incrementally increase the challenge. For example, if you are afraid to have a voice at the table in a work context, maybe ask to chair the meeting, co-present an idea or initiate a different forum or approach to the given agenda.

As we are more exposed to what we fear, our association with it starts to change. This is known as exposure therapy. By confronting what scares us, we build up our resilience to fear by inviting in opportunities and situations that could enrichen our life and that of others.

My questions to you

Think about what you are fearing and, above all, how your fear is holding you back.

- What is the cost of not facing what scares you?
- What is one step you can take towards exploring something you've been afraid of?

> *The human capacity for burden is like bamboo – far more flexible than you would ever believe at first glance.*
> —Jodi Picoult

Lyndelle's story

My sister, Lyndelle, is the poster child of resilience. She is not only my younger sister, but also my best friend.

She has battled depression since she was 19 years old, when she had a sudden nervous breakdown at the dinner table. She fought her depression head on, trying numerous medications, suffering addictions and having to stop work in her early 20s. Although she has been in and out of hospitals and rehabilitation centres and exposed to more doctors than you can imagine, she has always persevered to get through the dark times.

She has never complained or had a victim mentality. Instead, she gets on with things and uses her past challenges as fuel to drive her forward with a mindset so strong it blows me away. It has been challenging and sad for my family and me to witness her pain over the years, but one thing I have learnt is how strength can come from adopting a resilient mindset.

If these illnesses weren't enough, Lyndelle was diagnosed with aggressive breast cancer in March 2019. Even on the day of her diagnosis she was as selfless as ever, asking me to go about my life as usual.

As I write, she has had over 16 months of invasive chemotherapy, hormone therapy and immunotherapy, and a double mastectomy, all while still dealing with depression. We hope the worst is over now she is having preventative cancer treatment. She has handled the treatments with such grace and strength that even the doctors have praised her.

So many things make up resilience, including perseverance, gratitude, energy, mindset, courage and confidence. I wanted insight into the way Lyndelle handles her challenges, so I asked her. This in itself was challenging, as she doesn't like to be the centre of attention or have the focus on her. Here's how our conversation went:

Renée: Resilience doesn't mean you don't experience distress, sadness or difficulty. What does resilience mean to you?

Lyndelle: For me it's about taking each day as it comes, and dealing with things as they come up. Most of the time, it is unpleasant and challenging and I remind myself I have been dealt these cards, so there is no point complaining or burdening others. It's a strength to keep going and be here, some days. It's internal for me, a drive to keep going.

Renée: How have you been able to deal with such major challenges in your life and keep going?

Lyndelle: I've never seen myself as a victim, so I am never angry or resentful. I'll be the first to admit that a few challenging times were due to the choices I made that weren't resourceful. I try to focus on changing the things I can control. I don't have much energy from all the cancer treatment so I prioritise what I do, which is mainly treatment and doctors' appointments. I find not talking about things too much helps me get on with life instead of focusing on the negative. I do journal in my diary, only brief entries, and that helps a bit too.

Renée: What do you find the most challenging?

Lyndelle: The main things are lack of energy and feeling so tired all the time, the frustration of not knowing if I am clear of cancer, and the financial stress due to not being able to work. Not having energy means I can't do much and I feel like I'm letting people down, and many don't really understand and then I feel bad. Having treatment but not being clear and not knowing when that will be leaves a huge gap of uncertainty like I'm on a treadmill. Not working over the years has been hard and although I have some support this makes me feel guilty sometimes. I think overall the challenge is feeling frustrated that I can't lead what many call a 'normal' life and I miss out on so many things.

Renée: What do you tell yourself to keep your spirits up?

Lyndelle: Taking it one day at a time helps me from becoming overwhelmed. I focus on the moment, opposed to overthinking and even researching things. Reading magazines, watching TV and seeing family and close friends keep me occupied.

Functioning well involves the ability to overcome difficulties, to take risks, and to connect to other people. If children and adolescents feel include and accepted, particularly by a larger peer group, they are more likely to feel positive about themselves. —Berndt 1992; Hartup 2000

The resilience threshold

Throughout my life I had learnt to compartmentalise my work and my feelings. That was, until 10 days after hearing my sister's news about her breast cancer. I was coaching and mentoring a senior leader I have worked with for many years. Twenty minutes into the session, he brought up something I would normally delve into and challenge to get to an outcome. For the first time ever, after coaching thousands of clients, I just couldn't be present or in service.

My mind was struggling to comprehend what he was saying without comparing it to what my sister was going through. I judged his issue to be trivial in the scheme of things and kindly stood up and explained I would have to postpone the session. This client didn't know anything about my sister and after asking if I was okay, he walked me out. I sat in my car for about 15 minutes, shocked I had left yet also proud of myself.

I had hit what I call a 'resilience threshold', where I had reached a point in which I was so overwhelmed I couldn't be in service to my client. It went against all that I stand for and value in my work. This defining moment forced me to tap into the skills I've outlined in this chapter to work through the situation. It also made me realise how much adopting a Gift Mindset can help when we are faced with difficult and challenging situations.

Like the wrapping on a gift, it's the layers that offer protection and resilience is no different. The collection of traits, qualities and skills we learn through hardship become amour that can make us stronger and better equipped as time goes by.

Now it's time to unwrap your GIFT of Resilience

Take some time to think about the questions below.

G Grow

- What key lessons has the gift taught you?
- In what ways has it helped you to learn and grow?

I Integrate

- How will you incorporate these lessons into your life moving forward?
- What do you need to be aware of and what could get in the way of you actioning these lessons?

F Facilitate

- What lessons from this gift can you share with others professionally or personally?
- Who will you share these with and how will you share this gift?

T Transform

- How will you know that this gift has transformed you and others?
- When will you share this gift with others?

Your Resilience Bomboniera

- Develop an optimistic attitude and belief system to sustain and empower you, and propel you forward. Know who and what motivates you and lights you up – this can energise you during challenging times.
- Foster an attitude of gratitude every day – this has the power to heal, energise and bring hope. Tap into the skills and qualities that have helped you confront challenges in the past.
- Reframe a crisis, mistake or failure as a challenge: practise expressive writing for 20 minutes a day for four days and find three positives in every challenge. Make this a habit in a way that works for you.
- Focus your energy and time where you can have the most impact and influence, such as in building supportive relationships – they help us to face challenges. Tap into the resources, be it people or things, that will assist you to progress forward.
- Confront what scares you. Facing our fears helps us build resilience by slowly exposing ourselves to these things repeatedly.

Ten

THE GIFT OF GRATITUDE

> *Let us rise up and be thankful, for if we didn't learn a lot today, at least we learned a little, and if we didn't learn a little, at least we didn't get sick, and if we got sick, at least we didn't die; so, let us all be thankful.* —Buddhist teaching

In this chapter we will deep-dive into gratitude, the payoffs when we live a life of gratitude and how to practise gratitude as a daily part of life.

We will unwrap:

- the key obstacles that can prevent us from living in gratitude
- the five keys of gratitude – the HEART model
- the GIFT process to unwrap your Gift of Gratitude and share it.

But first, I'd like to share an amazing story taken from an interview I did with Claire Summers of Gratitude Glass Jars on the Limitless Leaders podcast. I met Claire back in my corporate life in 2004 and we reconnected around the time I was writing this book. Claire's story is based on creating a purpose-driven business that focuses on this gift.

Claire's story

Claire created the gratitude glass jar to help herself heal after experiencing a series of traumatic life events within seven months – she nursed her dad to his death through cancer, spent 11 days in intensive care with IVF complications, was sexually harassed at a 'dream job' in the US, suffered a miscarriage and had an ugly separation from her fiancé. This chain of events resulted in what Claire describes as 'beyond depression' – she felt total apathy, lost weight, became agoraphobic and began looking for the negative in situations and people.

In this dark time, Claire realised she hadn't created or released something within her – her gift to the world. It also hit home that she hadn't started a family. She was put on antidepressants, which she went off after two weeks as they were stifling her self-awareness.

Throughout this time, she found solace by writing down one or two things she was grateful for on folded-over cards. Being a visual person, she sketched the idea of a glass jar modelled on a vase at her mum's house. She began to place her gratitude notes into the vase. This became a visual cue and daily reminder that reinforced the good things in her life – things as simple as being able to go outside, enjoying a coffee or smiling at someone in the street.

Her daily notes of gratitude allowed her to see her abundance and regain faith in the world.

The summer it all changed

In the summer of 2017, Claire decided to exhibit at a trade show in New York to see if anyone would like her 'Gratitude Glass Jar' concept. This was a daring move, as she was up against huge brands. With only 300 jars manufactured, she won the award for the best product in the gift and lifestyle category. If that wasn't enough, she was hand-selected by the team at Oprah for consideration within Oprah's favourite things. Within eight weeks of launching the Gratitude Glass Jar she found herself on stage with Oprah Winfrey sharing her story. It was a life-changing moment. The product became the number-one-selling product on Amazon and appeared on TV and other media.

Gratitude Glass Jars has since developed into a lifestyle brand with an assortment of products that encourage people to pause, share their stories and inspire others. The global movement is based on capturing the spirit of living, celebrating life events, sharing memories and expressing words of love. Claire believes life is short, words go unsaid and values are not always lived.

Living gratitude every day

Here are Claire's top ways to drive gratitude in your life:

- Journal regularly about what you are grateful for.
- Reflect on what comes up for you – this reinforces the positives.
- Look for three positives as often as you can, opening up all your senses.
- Find a tool that works for you – creating a vision board, having a word of the day, journalling or even writing letters to yourself or others.
- Create a place to anchor gratitude, such as a 'just be' space in your house or at work, within a meeting or part of your morning ritual.

I love that Claire believes in sharing our stories openly – people learn, connect and attract other like-minded people. Her range of tools helps people assess themselves and live their best lives through gratitude.

As you can see, the Gift of Gratitude is one that Claire lives every day, and we can all access this by being mindful, open and focused on what we have, as opposed to what's missing. We need to be honest with ourselves, assess our lives and find ways to be grateful that suit us individually.

Gratitude in a nutshell

When I asked Claire what gratitude meant to her, she said she has always been a grateful person. She believes it is appreciating what you have, not just about looking at something you admire.

'Gratitude' is not a throwaway word – it lies within our heads and heart and it can force us to look at the world with a sense of beauty, childlike wonder and authenticity.

It shouldn't have to take a near-death experience to be grateful. Many people in developing countries have no material belongings, yet they seem to have a deeper sense of gratitude for their lives than many people in Western culture. The message here seems to be that if you and your family are in good health, that is enough; be grateful for life.

We can be grateful for many things in our lives such as certain people and situations, although most benefits come from others – hence gratitude is known as 'other-oriented'. It can mean different things to different people, depending on the context. Is gratitude an emotion? A behaviour or virtue? Research suggests that gratitude is not simply a cultural construct but is instead rooted in our evolutionary history, our DNA and in child development.

The experience of gratitude encourages us to appreciate what is good in our lives and compels us to pay this goodness forward.

I believe there are three main conduits to gratitude:

1. through our actions, such as sending a gift or saying thank you
2. through our feelings, where we feel grateful for something or someone

3. by adopting a grateful mindset, where we can see a positive experience within a challenge.

Gratitude is like the social glue that can fortify relationships between friends, family and life partners. It serves as a backbone to human society. Where I see organisations practise gratitude regularly by creating activities and forums to share, I observe people who are more generous, kind and wanting to build strong relationships.

We need to 'feel into' gratitude – something often missed in today's busy world. The pace at which we live and workplaces fostering a 'performance culture' can stifle the Gift of Gratitude.

Gratitude is a key driver to being resilient – when we focus on the good, we stop looking at what isn't there and the scarcity mentality dissipates.

Why can gratitude be challenging?

Claire believes that for us to be in true gratitude we need to stop and assess our life. This can be confronting and is something many of us avoid. People find it challenging to be honest with themselves about their lives, relationships and work because of the power of what it may mean and the change it may bring. Gratitude comes from thoughts and feelings deep in your soul. You cannot manufacture it – you would feel like a fraud if you did.

If we never stop and reflect, we risk living on autopilot. This is not a sustainable way to live our best life. Looking back, Claire realised that she was living on autopilot and she strongly believes this is where she went wrong in her own life; she went off track for three years, running with what she intuitively felt was wrong but was too afraid to act on. She believes this is where many people critically go wrong, when they could be living a life of higher self-awareness, gratitude and authenticity.

How does gratitude work?

To be in gratitude we need to reinforce what we already know. This can come from both positive and negative experiences. In Claire's case, going through numerous crises within a short timeframe forced her to go deep and try different ways to heal.

Gratitude works by reinforcing the positives, no matter how small, as this activates other senses such as smell, taste and touch. We then start to be open to receive more of what we have through more than one sense, thus building further positive experiences. Claire suggests finding three positive things in your day, week, month or life so when you are confronted with a negative experience you are ready to work through it and build your resilience.

Resilience and gratitude go hand in hand. The stronger the foundations of your gratitude habit, the easier it is to deal with any knockback.

Some psychologists categorise three types of gratitude:

1. **An 'affective trait':** A person's overall tendency to have a grateful disposition.
2. **A mood:** Where we have daily fluctuations in gratitude.
3. **An emotion:** A temporary feeling of gratitude, such as after receiving a gift.

I believe we get what we focus on and give our attention to, so we need to open our minds, hearts and intuition. Claire suggests when we are deep in gratitude we are also in contribution, which is one of the 12 Gifts of the Gift Mindset.

> *Your visions will become clear only when you can look into your own heart. Who looks outside, dreams; who looks inside, awakes.* — Carl Jung

The practice of gratitude is vital in all areas of life. It can take place as a feeling, a mindset or an action. Putting the Gift Mindset into practice, where you share the lessons of your challenges and successes, is a way to demonstrate gratitude and contribute to the culture in the workplace and at home.

Key obstacles to gratitude

It is important to be aware of the key obstacles that prevent us from living the Gift of Gratitude. As with anything in life, if we can be aware of what gets in the way we can be better prepared to combat it. There are many obstacles but I've outlined a few key ones here.

Lack of self-reflective time

Many people don't make the time to reflect and therefore aren't always aware of the gratitude that they could bring into their lives. By not taking the time, we may not be aware of the actual process to live with gratitude and therefore can't see the benefits. As human beings we can have a bias towards action and therefore don't prioritise quiet reflection time. Many people feel that self-reflective time is self-indulgent and this is where we need to question what it will cost us *not* to step back and make the time to practise gratitude.

Our attitude to gratitude

We can become complacent: the more we have and attain, the less grateful we become and we end up taking what we do have for granted. We can also carry a story of entitlement that we live by. This is where we believe we deserve things from other people or that thanking someone could be seen as a sign of weakness. We need to be aware of our pride, ego and relationship with gratitude, and how this is playing out.

Grey gratitude

Not being specific when expressing gratitude dilutes the impact and intention. Imagine replacing 'I'm grateful for that' with 'I'm grateful for the support you have given the team and me this month'. Examples and specifics prevent gratitude from being vague and ambiguous, or grey and unimpactful. Take the time to delve into what you are really grateful for and express that.

Cultural norms

The collective workplace culture can really drive whether the organisation is one that shares and shows gratitude. Not all companies embrace gratitude, and many are transaction- and performance-focused. Many people feel awkward showing gratitude and see it as a sign of weakness. Others believe that it is time-consuming, or fear they might not receive gratitude in return.

In our home lives, different backgrounds, experiences and ethnicity can play a huge role as far as the level of priority that gratitude is given. The good news is you have the choice in and out of work to make gratitude part of your life in a way that works for you.

Gratitude at work

If you are a leader who wants to encourage your employees to go beyond the contractual obligation of their roles, expressing gratitude should be part of your leadership. Gratefully acknowledging the thoughts and efforts of your people shows them that they matter, and this can also build a vital culture around gratitude.

In any role at work we should practise gratitude – this is the best way to ingrain it in your organisational culture. Research led by Lea Waters at the University of Melbourne found a positive relationship between expressing gratitude and increased productivity and job satisfaction. Gratitude can lower stress and reduce absenteeism.

In the workplace, gratitude may be expressed by a simple thankyou or pat on the back, or a deeper action such as creating activities to foster ongoing opportunities. Finding out how your people like to express and receive gratitude works best.

Benefits of gratitude

There are many benefits of gratitude. Robert Emmons, the world's leading scientific expert on gratitude, studied more than 1000 people from ages eight to 80, and found that people who practise gratitude consistently report a host of benefits:

- **Physical:**
  - Stronger immune systems
  - Less bothered by aches and pains
  - Lower blood pressure
  - Exercise more and take better care of their health
  - Sleep longer and feel more refreshed upon waking
- **Psychological:**
  - Higher levels of positive emotions
  - More alert, alive and awake
  - More joy and pleasure
  - More optimism and happiness
- **Social:**
  - More helpful, generous and compassionate
  - More forgiving
  - More outgoing
  - Feel less lonely and isolated

The social benefits are especially significant here because, after all, gratitude is a social emotion. I see it as a relationship-strengthening emotion because it requires us to see how we've been supported and affirmed by other people.

Some researchers also refer to an additional benefit of gratitude, known as the 'find-remind-bind' function. By attuning people to the thoughtfulness of others, gratitude helps them 'find' people who are good candidates for quality future relationships. It also helps 'remind' people of the goodness of their existing relationships.

Lastly, it 'binds' them to their partners and friends by making them feel appreciated, and encouraging them to engage in behaviour that will help prolong their relationships.

HEART – the five key drivers of gratitude

Gratitude is something I practise regularly. It helps keep me focused in business and in life and layers into my resilience, especially when things get tough.

I have developed a five-step process with the acronym HEART.

Gratitude is the fairest blossom which springs from the soul.
—Henry Ward Beecher

H – Harness

Firstly, you need to harness the power of gratitude – you choose to be grateful, someone who sees the positive and negative in their life as gifts and takes the time to be aware of them. You need to know what gratitude means to you and discover what you are grateful for.

Make the time and create the headspace and environment to be in gratitude, both in the workplace and at home. Find a way or process to capture what you are grateful for. It could be choosing a time of day to write down who and what you are grateful for. However you do this will build a grateful disposition within you – in time, it will become a part of who you are.

Find three key positives each day. Focus on what you are grateful for, what you do have. Be specific and include the detail of why you are grateful. Capture your sources of gratitude in a way that works for you.

E – Express

When we express gratitude, we are releasing our thoughts and feelings. You need to express gratitude in your own way and sit with it.

Firstly, you need to be specific and articulate what exactly you are grateful for:

- What was the best thing that has happened today, this week, this month?
- Who is/are the person/s you are most grateful for?
- Why are you grateful for these people and things?

Expressing gratitude to others could be in the form of a thankyou note, a phone call, an email, a passing comment, deeply listening to someone or even taking someone out for a coffee or lunch. In a study, the Happiness Project found that when thankyou letters were sent in the post the 'happiness level' went from 2% to 4%. When people were phoned directly, this increased by 4% to 19%.

Here are a few ideas for expressing gratitude in the workplace:

- During team meetings, share what each of you has learnt and enjoyed from working with each other.
- Send surprise emails to others expressing appreciation.
- Create a forum to share internal updates and encourage people to share.

It is important to think of subtle ways of sharing gratitude every day within the workplace. Ideally, there will be structured forums to share as well as spontaneous recognition and ways to show appreciation. Be mindful not to do 'gratitude' in overdrive – this can seem false and dilute the effects of authentically being grateful.

A – Anchor

Once you have expressed gratitude, anchor it as a habit and a practice. An anchor is a trigger or stimulus that retrieves a desired emotional state.

The more we tap into this state, the stronger the anchor becomes. For example, listening to a certain song may remind you of someone you are grateful to know, or smelling a certain scent may remind you of a holiday where you felt grateful to be alive.

By anchoring what we are grateful for through senses such as touch, taste, sight and smell, we can tap into a particular emotion or feeling. I believe anchoring gratitude helps us look for what we are grateful for every day, as opposed to gratitude being a one-off practice.

Anchoring is a powerful way to reinforce gratitude in our lives to help us deal with challenges and setbacks. Here's how to do it:

- Identify what or whom you are grateful for – be specific.
- Decide on how you will anchor this: a thought, feeling, visual, smell or sound.
- Relive the feeling of gratitude and appreciation – 'feel into' it.
- Repeat this process often.

R – Reassess

Take the time to reflect and reassess what is working in your practice of gratitude – what fuels you and makes you feel grateful. Gratitude requires us to reassess our lives and all within them: our relationships, work, self-growth and so on. This forces us to consider different factors and see things in a new light.

Gratitude shouldn't be a throwaway word, but instead an ongoing practice that we review and renew. The things we are grateful for may change as we, and the situations around us, change. Ensure you take the time to reassess, both in the workplace and in your personal life.

T – Thankful

Be thankful for what you have done and how it has made you and others feel. Both being grateful and thankful are triggered by a situation, event or person and both are linked. I believe gratitude is usually directed outwardly, while thankfulness is generated within us. It only takes a moment to be thankful.

Some simple ideas for thankfulness:

- Notice beauty in nature each day.
- Compliment work colleagues on the fly.
- Let a friend or colleague know what they mean to you.
- Be thankful for the growth opportunity challenges bring.
- Be grateful for the small things we sometimes take for granted.
- Spend quality time with the people you love.
- Be thankful for learning something new.

Invest in moments to be thankful for – this will ensure you create a consistent loop of building, expressing and living the Gift of Gratitude in your life.

We all have stories to share of what we are grateful for. Remember, our gifts can be in the present or in the past, or may be hidden and take some time to unwrap.

Now it's time to unwrap your GIFT of Gratitude

Take some time to think about the questions below.

G Grow

- What key lessons has the gift taught you?
- In what ways has it helped you to learn and grow?

I Integrate

- How will you incorporate these lessons into your life moving forward?
- What do you need to be aware of and what could get in the way of you actioning these lessons?

F Facilitate

- What lessons from this gift can you share with others professionally or personally?
- Who will you share these with and how will you share this gift?

T Transform

- How will you know that this gift has transformed you and others?
- When will you share this gift with others?

Your Gratitude Bomboniera

- Gratitude is about appreciating what you have and paying this goodness forward. It can be in the form of an action, a feeling or having a grateful disposition and mindset.
- To stop and assess our lives can be confronting to many people, so it's often avoided. We need to be open and honest with ourselves and reassess our work and relationships.
- Gratitude works by reinforcing the positives, even when experiencing something negative. The stronger the foundations of what you are grateful for, the easier it is to deal with any knockback.
- Find three key positives each day by focusing on what you are grateful for and what you do have – be specific as to the details. Find a space where you can capture and express this.
- To practise gratitude, apply the five keys of gratitude (HEART model) – Harness gratitude; Express it; Anchor it and Reassess what you are grateful for; Thankful moments create a gratitude loop.

Eleven

THE GIFT OF CURIOSITY

> *I think, at a child's birth, if a mother could ask a fairy godmother to endow it with the most useful gift, that gift should be curiosity.* —Eleanor Roosevelt

In this chapter, we will explore what it means to be curious and how curiosity can shape our decisions, outcomes and lives. We will expand on the ways we can foster a curious mindset and tap into the gift of curiosity.

We will unwrap:

- the curiosity mindset
- the four keys to curiosity
- my gift of curiosity
- the GIFT process to unwrap your Gift of Curiosity and share it.

But first, I'd like to share how the gift of curiosity shaped a business opportunity for Kate Stewart, founder of Stay Tray.

Kate's story

Stay Tray is a small business with big dreams and a lofty purpose: to reduce waste in the world by encouraging good habits in our community through the use of a humble beverage tray.

Spending most of her career working with major retailers in fast-moving consumer goods, Kate witnessed copious amounts of waste. This prompted a career change in the pursuit of something more fulfilling.

Stay Tray is a sustainable solution to reducing single-use containers, made in Australia from 100% recycled material.

The concept was one of those things sitting in the back of Kate's mind. She knew her idea was needed, with the global focus on sustainability and decreasing single-use products. Seeing people going to and from cafés doing the coffee run, with so many using reusable coffee cups but then placing them in a single-use cardboard tray, Kate knew this didn't make any sense. She felt there was opportunity to rethink this space. That is when her curiosity came into play and led her in a direction she could never have imagined.

Soon after her initial idea, Kate researched to check that no-one else was producing a recycled tray. To her astonishment, no-one was – let alone one Australian-made. The focus now was to work out how she could produce the tray in Australia, instead of going to China as many do. Kate's curious mind opened up the possibility of utilising the world's recycled waste. It was an interesting journey that has seen Stay Tray divert more than 4 billion takeaway cups from landfill at the time this book was written.

Kate believes her business is where it is today because she kept asking questions. Her favourite question to ask when faced with a challenge or roadblock is, 'Why not?'

Curiosity is ...

Kate believes that curiosity is about exploring. Curiosity fuels passion and learning and creates possibility. Curiosity requires people to think differently. It's about not accepting the norm and the present state.

A curious mindset can lead you anywhere – in fact, being curious can create too many possibilities. Kate believes that you need to explore and then rechannel and focus to work out your direction.

We bring to life the things that we are curious about by the choices we make. A curious mindset sets us up to innovate and look at possibilities with an open mind.

Curiosity fuels provocation, passion and learning, Kate says – and I couldn't agree more. Provocation gets people to assess a situation, object or environment. It is the key to curiosity and thinking differently.

We need to get out of our comfort zone in order to be curious. Innovation would not have come about if Kate hadn't observed her environment and the way people were behaving. Taking the time to reflect and assess things opens up opportunities to be curious, she says.

Curiosity drives resilience

Curiosity is a key skill of resilience, Kate says, along with others such as gratitude. If we are willing to have an open mind and think differently, a habit of questioning and trying new things can improve the way in which we approach both opportunities and challenges.

Curiosity in leadership

Kate believes agility and innovation come from having a curious mindset. When we question things outside of what we know, change and creativity increase.

Great coaches and leaders challenge the norm and ask thought-provoking questions such as 'what if?' and 'why not?' Great leaders support their people and provide all the assets required for them to do their jobs. They lead with provocation around 'do we accept that as the normal?' The best leaders Kate has worked with have a curious mindset and immerse themselves in that space – that's where they thrive.

Challenges

There are challenges with any business, and Kate's initial challenge was navigating moving from the corporate world, where resources and processes were on tap, to being on her own in a new industry she knew nothing about. It helped her to control what she could and, through curiosity, seek out the support that she needed. She reached out to her contacts and network, asked questions and was open to feedback. She was excited by the opportunity and the chance to learn.

Not everyone has a curious mindset

Curiosity can sometimes be exhausting, and Kate knows this well, having an inquisitive six-year-old child. She knows other people and leaders, though, who have people in their teams who aren't very curious and don't ask many questions. As leaders, they may feel frustrated with this, so they try to coach that individual or probe them for more information through simple questions such as, 'How might something be done differently?'

Some people are afraid of delving into the unknown and curiosity is not their strength. Kate believes we aren't all born with curiosity – it is a trait we can develop when we are passionate about something. It's not everyone's first preference to be curious. I think leaders can have day-to-day conversations with their team, peers or others in the industry and pretty much work out where someone is on the scale of curiosity. Fear, societal norms and values, family and having automated ways of doing things, such as technology, can hold us back from being curious.

Kate says that probing people to think differently and asking questions to find out more can increase curiosity. People who accept things the way they are may get scared of getting something wrong and what this may mean. The best leaders Kate has worked with exude curiosity and empathy as key traits and I agree with this, as I learnt the most from leaders who adopted the gift of curiosity.

Kate's three key tips to bring more curiosity into your life

The value of the Gift of Curiosity is it can lead us in unexpected directions, as it did for Kate. Had she never questioned her idea and explored it further, the Stay Tray wouldn't exist today. Here are her three key tips to develop your curiosity:

1. **Explore:** Ramp up your curiosity by focusing on a passion you have. Explore something you're interested in – a potential side hustle or an idea.
2. **Be agile and innovative:** Adopt a curious mindset that will drive this.
3. **Create the space:** Stop, pause and take stock of what you are doing and why. Invest in critical thinking time that will open your mind up.

What is curiosity?

I believe curiosity is an important genius trait. Imagine if Leonardo da Vinci, Walt Disney, Thomas Edison, Albert Einstein or Richard Feynman had been afraid of asking questions?

> *The important thing is not to stop questioning …*
> *Never lose a holy curiosity.* —Albert Einstein

Curiosity is a skill and also a characteristic – a motivated desire for more information. It's the engine that drives learning and achievement, and it's almost like a state of arousal that needs to be provoked. Being curious requires us to ask questions of ourselves, situations and others. This helps us grow and be what I call 'in flow'.

Ask to know
Know to grow
Grow to be in flow.

Dr Daniel Berlyne was a pioneer in curiosity research in the '60s. His work in the field of experimental and exploratory psychology has served as the foundational research for many scientists who have followed. He stated that curiosity is innate to our being, not unlike food and water. He also concluded that it is instigated by three key sources:

1. **Novelty:** Things that are new or unknown to us.
2. **Ambiguity:** Things that are confusing to us.
3. **Complexity:** Things that are partially known to us that we seek to know more about.

All these sources of curiosity surround us – it's up to us to raise our emotional intelligence, be aware of them, then decide on what to do next.

State or trait curiosity

Curiosity originates either outside us – state curiosity – or inside us – trait curiosity.

For example, observing something out of the ordinary such as a magic trick might evoke a fleeting moment of curiosity – state curiosity – based on an external situation. This type of curiosity can be related to high levels of excitement or reward.

Trait curiosity is a characteristic within all of us, but it's only exhibited in a high order in some people. A key characteristic of trait curiosity is having a lifelong interest in learning. Trait curiosity can be stifled due to anxiety, fear and social norms.

A good way to look at curiosity is the urge or drive that takes us out of our comfort zone to know more, based on the interests that we choose to pursue.

> *Give people facts and you feed their minds for an hour.*
> *Awaken curiosity, and they feed their own minds for a lifetime.*
> —Ian Russell

The curiosity model

Curiosity is both a mindset and a process that involves exploring three key steps. This is a process I have developed that I use personally and with many clients looking to explore and expand their curiosity to ramp up innovation, learning and creativity as a team.

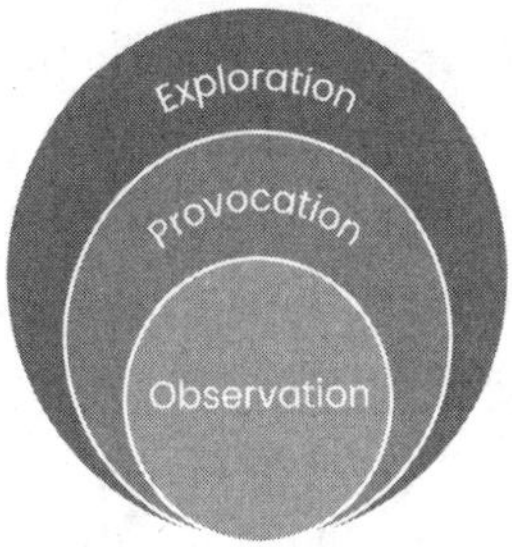

Observation

Take the time and create the space to stop, pause and observe where you are at. What object, situation, person or idea are you curious about? Maybe it's an unanswered question, something you've ignored in the past or a passion you've swept under the carpet. Use all your senses to consider this.

You could be observing something that's within you – trait curiosity – or something you would like to explore further – state curiosity.

Provocation

In the context of curiosity, provocation is the act of provoking and stimulating different ways of thinking and new ideas. Now is the time to probe around what you need to know, what could be done, what could be challenged. I believe provocation takes energy and commitment and can be a good litmus test to validate the importance of what you are curious about. Think about what you need to know in your leadership or life and the questions you need to ask to find this out.

Exploration

This requires action – it is the exciting, progressive part of curiosity. Exploration helps us expand our knowledge and the best way to do this is to ask questions of yourself, others and situations. Research by reading, having conversations, questioning and challenging and almost irritating the status quo. Take in your thoughts and all outside feedback and stay focused on your curiosity. Asking 'why?' or 'why not?' can open up new thinking from others and create new questions for you. A great tip when you think of something: turn a statement into a question. This will help you explore more and not just have a one-dimensional thought. For example, I could admire someone and think, *Wow, that person is amazing* or I could flip this into a question and ask myself, 'I wonder how they do what they do?' This opens up my thinking to explore, learn and find out more.

> *Always question the why … don't be satisfied with only knowing the how.* —Catherine Pulsifer

The four keys to curiosity

Let's take a look at the four skills needed to develop your curiosity.

1. Have an open mind

This takes discipline. The more open you are, the more likely you will be able to receive new information and ideas that can help you continue to be curious.

Avoid closing yourself off; instead, stretch yourself out of your safe zone – anything outside this is growth. Don't be afraid to ask questions; stay present when listening. I ask myself, 'What can I learn from this person?' – this opens up my mind to receive and not discount others' ideas or opinions.

2. Ask questions

This helps you become a more effective communicator, as well as build stronger relationships and leadership capability. Asking questions with intention is a great way to understand, seek information and explore your curiosity in the process. And don't forget to question yourself and the things you do and think – this is something a lot of us miss.

Whether you are questioning another person, yourself or a situation, asking open questions is key. An open question is one where the answer can't be 'yes' or 'no'. It's a great way to elicit information and get the other person talking. After choosing open questions, you can then drill down with closed questions.

Open questions begin with *who, what, where, when, why* and *how*. Some call them the five wives and the one husband – this always helped me remember them! Think of open questions as being at the top of the questioning funnel where you are probing to get lots of information.

Asking open questions is challenging as we tend to do two things:

1. Think ahead and ask a closed question to get to our point.
2. Ask more than one question at a time to lead to what we want to talk about.

A key tip to asking open questions is to add 'tell me about' to the start of your questions – this will turn them intoan open questions.

When we ask curious open questions, we need to be open to not knowing the answer, and not assume or judge. Our intention should be to focus on learning and understanding more.

Curious questions include:

- What do I/you think of this idea?
- How could this work?
- Why do I/you think this idea could work?
- What could go right and wrong?
- What would I/you do if there were no limitations and unlimited time and resources?
- What is a great question I could ask you right now?
- What else?

Another technique is to flip statements into questions. When we think about something, we articulate it in our minds as either a statement or a question. For example, flipping a statement such as 'What that team did was great' to 'I wonder how that team achieved that?' will change your energy and provoke questioning and conversations. It changes a one-dimensional thought to a two-dimensional question.

Take the time to observe the statements you think or write, such as in an email, and flip these into questions.

3. Listen and be present

Listening is one of the most challenging skills to master. Communication isn't just about what you say – it is 50% speaking and 50% listening.

Research has found that only 2% of leaders have ever received any training on how to listen, and most people struggle to listen and not just 'hear'.

As human beings we aren't wired to listen, although it is one of the first things we learn in our mother's womb. We think at more than 400 words a minute and speak at 150, so it's no wonder our minds wander when we should be listening.

Here are some ways you can actively work on your listening skills:

- Watch people's mouths as they speak; this can help keep you present.
- Ask questions one at a time, and create your next question based on the response you receive (rather than formulating your next question in your mind while the other person is talking).
- When there is silence, don't feel you need to fill the gap; count to 10 (in your head) and usually someone else will talk.
- Remember to listen to what is *not* being said.
- Pay attention to non-verbal cues such as tone, pitch and base of voice, and body language.

To be truly curious we need to listen to:

- ourselves, both logically and intuitively
- the responses of others, without bias or judgement
- situations that present themselves
- thoughts, feedback and feelings through all our senses.

4. Be interested

Reframe 'boring' situations and people to 'interesting'. A simple reframe can change your energy, attitude and ability to be curious. We can learn much from others if we have an open mind and question things.

I read a great story many years ago. A woman prepared a lamb roast each Sunday night for her family. Her husband used to cut the leg of lamb in half before roasting it, and one afternoon he asked his wife, 'Why do we cut the leg of lamb in half?' She responded, 'I have no idea, we have always done it that way.' Wiping her apron, pondering her husband's question, she called her mum to ask. Her mum, puzzled, responded with, 'I don't know, maybe ask your grandmother.' Highly curious now, the woman set aside the vegetables she was cutting and called her grandmother. 'Nanna, why do you, Mum and I cut our Sunday leg of lamb in half?' The grandmother replied, 'Well, I've always cut mine in half as I had a small oven.' The woman burst out laughing as she looked at her 900mm oven.

Sometimes the simple tasks and decisions are carried out in autopilot. Often, we become time-poor and miss opportunities.

When the stakes are high and the pressure is on, it can be difficult for leaders, especially senior ones new to their roles, to pause before acting, take a step back and reflect on why they are doing what they are doing. This also applies to those around them.

Sometimes questioning our actions on the bigger things can be hampered by our inaction on questioning the smaller things.

My Gift of Curiosity

In my corporate life, I was always looking at ways to grow and develop my team, myself and those around me. I've always had a growth mindset and, luckily for me, I worked in an organisation that was supportive of developing their people.

While in a senior leadership role, I faced the challenge of having to manage upwards in order to gain buy-in and support to implement initiatives my team and I were working on. My direct manager wasn't a strong leader and tended to do things the way they were always done, not being open to change and new ways.

After questioning the way things were done, I knew I had to upskill. This forced me to explore coaching, mentoring and other self-development tools, both in and out of work time, in order to manage my relationship and the conversations I had with my manager.

In the process, I became hooked on developing others. This curiosity has led me to where I am now. If I had adopted a 'status quo' mindset, my life and that of many others would be different now.

This experience taught me the value of the Gift of Curiosity.

Curiosity could be a past, present, hidden or future gift that is waiting to be explored. Be aware of times that curiosity has served you well so you can reflect on the lessons and share them. Remember: curiosity can open up opportunities, direction and new ways of thinking and being in many parts of our lives.

Now it's time to unwrap your GIFT of Curiosity

Take some time to think about the questions below.

G Grow

- What key lessons has the gift taught you?
- In what ways has it helped you to learn and grow?

I Integrate

- How will you incorporate these lessons into your life moving forward?
- What do you need to be aware of and what could get in the way of you actioning these lessons?

F Facilitate

- What lessons from this gift can you share with others professionally or personally?
- Who will you share these with and how will you share this gift?

T Transform

- How will you know that this gift has transformed you and others?
- When will you share this gift with others?

Your Curiosity Bomboniera

- Focus on an interest or passion. Don't accept the norm or the state in which things exist. Provocation is the key to curiosity and thinking differently.
- Curiosity originates inside or outside of us – trait or state curiosity. A key characteristic of trait curiosity is having a lifelong interest in learning.
- Use my three-step curiosity model: observe, provoke, explore.
- Have an open mind and ask questions – be open to exploring possibilities and new learnings.
- Flip statements to questions to activate curiosity and open up possibility. Listen, be present and question things to remain interested and curious.

Twelve

THE GIFT OF CHANGE

If there was no change, we wouldn't have butterflies.
—Unknown

To unwrap the Gift of Change, we will explore how to embrace change and the reasons why, as humans, we usually resist it. We will then expand on key strategies to deal with any change, in both your professional and personal life.

We will unwrap:

- the idea of embracing unknown change
- eight keys to embrace change
- the GIFT process to help you unwrap your Gift of Change and share it.

But first, I'd like to share a story of two major changes that I faced in my career – one of my choosing, the other forced upon me. Despite the difference in how they came about, I dealt with both changes in similar ways.

The chosen change

It was February 2007, As I walked downstairs, I couldn't look back up at the office I'd given my heart and soul to for over 10 years. I'd decided to start my own business 12 months before and felt excited by the possibility, but now the thought of leaving the safe cocoon of the corporate world had me feeling empty, overwhelmed and afraid. Who knew you could have so many emotions at once? The committee in my head was full of questions:

- 'What are you doing?'
- 'How will you make it on your own?'
- 'Where is that next pay cheque coming from?'
- 'Aren't you going to miss all of your colleagues?'

Mind whirling, I got into my car in tears. On the radio, John Mayer's voice was amplified, singing 'Stop this train'. I took off down the driveway, the office getting smaller behind me, every kilometre bringing me closer to my next adventure.

My 'why' to change

Many of the people I worked with in the corporate world remain some of my closest friends. I loved the company, and still do. The leaders I had worked with – some amazing and some not-so-amazing – had given me experiences, learnings and gifts that still serve me. But deep down I knew I was ready to help people grow. I had held senior sales and leadership roles in corporate life. I knew the challenges of being a leader. During my last leadership role, I had spent every waking hour outside work studying coaching and neurolinguistic programming (NLP), among other things. I knew that I had something deeper to share with the world.

My dad was an entrepreneur and I'd always had that creative spirit, starting mini businesses as a teenager. Many people around me were not so supportive, warning of potential risk, but this made me even more determined. When self-doubt knocked at my door I flipped it, trying to focus on the opportunities to grow and learn.

I continued to read furiously, study at night, attend programs and coach anyone and anything; I think I even did a session with my dog, Jessie! I joined relevant associations and started my business initially coaching and mentoring executives one on one, growing as my clients grew.

Brave unknown change

It probably seems like everything was falling into place, but my husband and I were both self-employed – something I hadn't taken into consideration when leaving my secure job. I was still building my business and my husband was working 24/7 on knocking down an old house and developing two new dwellings. It felt like we were facing one issue after another. We were dodging bullets such as building objections, cash-flow issues and sleep deprivation, while I was trying to write IP, sell my programs and deliver them with my usual passion and commitment. My younger sister also became very ill with depression during this time, so we were in and out of hospitals giving her all the support that we could.

Due to us both being eternal optimists (plus a lot of hard work and family support), we got through. This time taught us both resilience, which has kept us strong through some pretty challenging times. It taught me that change requires sacrifice. Anyone who tells you running your own business is smooth sailing is either unaware or in denial.

I think being open to embracing what I call 'unknown change' with a focus on the 'why' of what we were both doing kept us motivated, enabling us to stay energised to overcome the obstacles (gifts) over those three years.

We could easily have resisted these changes and shut the building job down. I could have gone back to the corporate world. At times

I was tempted, but my 'why' to start my own business was larger than my 'why' to go back to what was familiar and easy. Our next life chapter could have been comfortable and harmonious. Instead, we stayed focused on the *reason* for what we were doing and braved whatever was thrown at us.

Change brings opportunity

During this challenging time, I came across an opportunity to run a program helping jobseekers back into the workforce. This was not part of my plan, but a great opportunity to learn, contribute and earn an income to fund our properties and keep them afloat. Change can bring other unexpected opportunities, and running this program built me into the person I am today – both personally and professionally, as an educator.

The programs ran for 10 days, often in remote places such as far north Australia. As exhausting as they were, they were also very rewarding and I ran them for over 15 months with extremely successful outcomes.

I have never been one to take anyone or anything for granted, but this experience took that belief to the next level. I learnt that people really do need to have a purpose, whether in life, in self or professionally. My purpose was to learn and grow by helping others grow. Seeing so many people get their lives back solidified my objectives in leaving the corporate world. I also realised first-hand that if you place people before progress, success will happen.

My business started to evolve and before long I was mentoring, coaching and running leadership and sales capability programs. Although the jobseeker training program ceased, I felt I had contributed to something bigger, which helped me stay focused on what I could control and influence.

We built the two townhouses and moved in – a huge relief and such an exciting time. Call us crazy, but we hosted Christmas Day for 35 people two days after moving in. It is amazing how the hard times can dissipate once you achieve what you set out to do. I remind myself of this when going through changes that aren't easy to accept or transition through. Remember, we can either resist or embrace change and it comes down to acceptance – a topic we dived into earlier in this book.

The forced change

Fourteen years on in my business, and here I am writing my third book in the middle of a global pandemic.

It's a Saturday afternoon, as I only write on the weekends. I started this book the week before COVID-19 reared its ugly head in Australia and turned the world upside down. As with many others, my business was affected, so this book had to become a weekend project as my weekdays and nights were consumed with saving my business.

In late March my business was set to have its best year ever. It was like I was accelerating along a highway when I was suddenly hit with a flat tyre and everything came to an abrupt halt. That's how it felt when over 80% of our clients postponed programs with us after the pandemic hit. This was understandable, but it created so much uncertainty about where my business was headed, among other things – including loved ones' health and our future.

Pre-COVID, we ran most of our workshops, coaching and speaking engagements face to face. This was what we were known for and what we passionately loved doing. The lockdown forced us to reimagine how we did what we did, as we weren't able to physically be in a room with our clients.

I can honestly say the panic, fear and overwhelm blanketed me for a day and then I asked myself, 'What can I focus on?' I reframed the word 'uncertainty' to 'focus' and the word 'pain' to 'purpose' and have not looked back. I knew the market would need what we had and that we just needed to change the 'how' of what we did.

In four weeks, I created an online program on leading and working remotely, staying in service to my clients, running many complimentary support webinars and sessions. We also had a key staff member move on for personal reasons. I recruited and trained three new people in smaller specialist roles, all through virtual conferencing. In 12 weeks, I had three days off and worked night and day against this forced change upon my business and my life.

Yesterday I was clever, so I wanted to change the world.
Today I am wise, so I am changing myself. —Rumi

What helped me was to focus on what we *could* do, rather than what we couldn't, which results in little action. This is key in progressing. Another thing I realised is that I am living on purpose in what I do professionally, and staying focused on that has kept my mindset in a progressive mode. Being a connector, working 24/7 from home for six months, I can say I've never been more connected. Using regular virtual catch-ups and phone conversations, I have tapped into what lights me up to stay motivated. Being grateful for what I do have, when so many people have suffered worse, has helped me stay in touch with what matters.

As I write this, Stage 4 lockdown restrictions in Victoria are still in place and, although there is still great uncertainty, one of the gifts throughout this change was that we started working with a few new clients. I can't deny I am looking forward to 'pressing the flesh' and working with clients in the same physical location, hopefully soon. At the same time, I have learnt so much about myself and my capability to deal with change, and have become closer to many clients, as tough as it has been.

Forced change is daunting but it can also bring so many gifts. This present Gift of Change has taught me that my mindset, self-belief and staying focused on what can be done is pivotal in any change I face in the future. These lessons are similar in a change you choose or a change that is forced upon you.

Your relationship with change

As you can see in my story, change is one of the few constants in life. Many people resist change, while others embrace it. I believe it all comes down to how you are wired and the reference and experience you associate with change. Certainty is a core human need, therefore it is natural to resist what is unknown to us. Change makes us feel uneasy as it takes us into the unknown and moves us away from the things we feel are certain. Change brings new choices that can create uncertainty, and uncertainty can stifle decisions.

Nineteenth-century French naturalist Jean-Henri Fabre experimented with pine processionary caterpillars, placing them in single file in a continuous loop around the rim of a flowerpot. Each caterpillar's head touched the one in front so they formed a circle. The caterpillars' favourite food was placed in the centre. Interestingly, the caterpillars moved around the circle for seven days, following the caterpillar in front of them, oblivious to the food they could access in the centre. Even though their food was less than 15 centimetres away from them, they all died of exhaustion and hunger. If only one had changed direction and accessed the food, they would have all survived. This is a great demonstration of how we can get caught up in doing what we have always done and not be open to change. Sometimes we miss what is right in front of us – we drive to work the same way, follow the same processes or simply avoid voicing our opinions, preferring to follow what has always been done before.

Change is an imperative in life. I believe it equates to growth, new learnings and possibilities. The Gift of Change, although sometimes forced and challenging, is needed if we are to move beyond stagnation.

Here are three questions you can ask yourself to gauge whether you are out of your comfort zone and open to change:

1. Is your 'why' to change exceeding your 'why' to stay the same?

2. How open are you being to identify and implement necessary changes?
3. What do you do that scares you and opens you up to new possibilities?

The changes we face in life can come in varying forms, both professionally and personally. The most successful people, leaders and business owners I know embrace unknown change and take risks to grow. They don't stay with what is comfortable – a trap that is easy to fall into.

I believe we can fall into one of four change patterns:

1. **Comfortable:** We embrace known change because it can feel safe and expected.
2. **Defiant:** We resist known change and many times don't understand the reason behind it.
3. **Fearful:** We resist unknown change as we usually don't understand the motivation behind it.
4. **Brave:** When we are brave for change, we are embracing the unknown and taking a risk to do so.

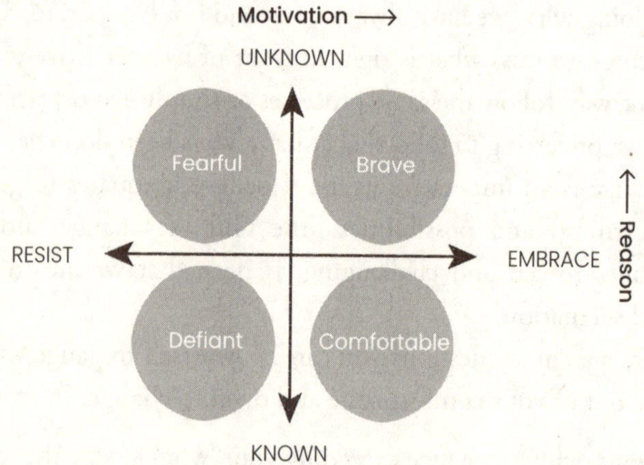

It's worth reflecting on where you sit, remembering you can move in and out of each quadrant, dependent on what is going on for you.

It is natural to embrace changes that are known and comfortable. To be open to the Gift of Change, I believe we need to open up our hearts and minds – both our logical and emotional sides. When we have a compelling reason to make a change (the 'why') and the motivation to make it happen, we are more likely to embrace it.

I love change and embracing the unknown; although not easy at times, being open to review and exploring the possibility of change has served me well. Forced or unknown change is always more challenging to deal with. My belief that things happen for a lesson is another insight that keeps me focused and open.

> *Change is hardest at the start, messiest in the middle and best at the end.* —Robin Sharma

The eight keys to embrace change

We all deal with change in our own way. Whether your Gift of Change and the lessons learnt are hidden, in the past or happening now, the following tried-and-tested tips will help you unwrap this gift.

1. Know the reason – the 'why' to change

Your 'why' to change must exceed your 'why' to stay the same.

Make sure your chosen change is happening for the right reason, especially when it is influenced by you. You will only embrace change or buy into it if there is something in it for you. Not embracing change is usually due to a lack of clarity around the reasons why. Take the time to understand the reasons for and benefit of the change.

When leading or sharing a change, ensure others understand the reason. Involve them in the process where you can, as people own what they co-create. I see many leaders focus on strategy, structure, culture and so on when they are leading through change. What they forget is to focus on the most important part of change: changing the behaviour of people. This is achieved by speaking to people's feelings and empowering them to create new habits related to the change.

2. Focus on what isn't *changing and what you can control*

As humans we naturally concentrate on what is changing. When dealing with change, it helps to focus on a few things that *aren't* changing. This gives you a sense of stability to help you deal with what is changing. For example, when going through a career change, choose to focus on things that are stable such as your exercise routine, time with loved ones and even your community. Look at things you can control and influence, such as habits and routines that serve you.

3. Find balance between the logical and the emotional

There's a great book called *Switch* by Dan and Chip Heath. It focuses on being on the same page with your emotional and rational sides when dealing with change. They use the example of the elephant (representing our emotional side) and the rider (representing our rational side). Our emotions can overwhelm our rational thoughts, in the same way as a large elephant could overwhelm a rider. But if we rely solely on rational behaviour, we can overthink things. Dan and Chip suggest directing the rider and motivating the elephant.

For example, maybe there is someone you work with who can brainstorm for hours but can't make a decision; this is the rider working in overdrive who needs to bring in more emotion (the elephant). They both work hand in hand, but there needs to be a conscious balance. Learning to respond and not react and adopting the elephant and rider analogy can help keep this is check.

4. Accept that change is a process

As with any process, you need to work through steps to get to an outcome. Being aware of these steps can enable you to move through change more quickly and, in the process, amplify self-awareness.

The model below displays the five steps we go through when dealing with any change in our personal or professional lives:

1. **Reflect:** This is where we question the situation and reflect on why it is happening.
2. **Recalibrate:** At this stage, we weigh up our readiness to deal with the change.
3. **Act:** This is where we do what is needed to accept and action the actual change.
4. **Align:** Here, we align our values, thoughts and actions to ourself and the situation.
5. **Preserve:** This is where we move on and maintain the change.

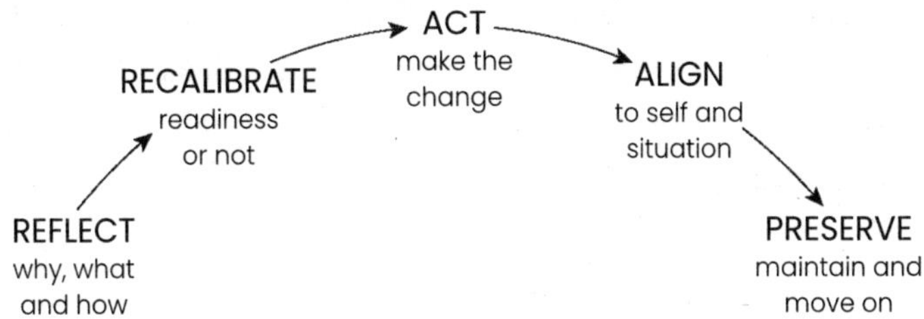

The model helps us live our Gift of Change and learn as we progress through it. Many of my clients and their teams reference this model, but we all move through the process at a different rate and intensity. It is helpful to know and appreciate where you and others are in order to support and move forward together.

5. Know what lights you up

Tap into the things that motivate you and make you feel alive. Doing what energises us can be used to fuel us through a change. When I was pivoting my business to online during the pandemic, I made sure I connected with others online and ran virtual workshops as much as I could, as I knew that connection is what would keep my energy up.

Remind yourself of the skills and mindset that have helped you deal with changes in the past. Anything you have done you can do again. I look at change, big or small, as a process that can be applied time and time again.

6. Be mindful of change effort

Change can be exhausting. The effort that goes into dealing with any change can affect us physically, mentally and emotionally, especially when going through a major change or more than one change at a time. It is known that large changes can zap our self-control and consequently our capacity to think, focus, be creative and persist becomes non-existent. It may look to others like you are resisting change or being lazy, when in actual fact you are worn out and can't function to deal with it yet.

> *Change is hard because people wear themselves out ...*
> *what looks like laziness is often exhaustion.* —Chip Heath

7. Avoid decision paralysis

Too many options can cause us to freeze up and default to doing nothing.

Think about a retail store crammed and overflowing with items or a dinner menu with endless options. We can get what I call 'decision fatigue' and end up not purchasing anything. I've been in work meetings where so many options and ideas are generated that people become overwhelmed and nothing gets actioned. As Barry Schwartz says in his book *The Paradox of Choice*, as we face more and more options, we become overloaded. Choice no longer liberates, it debilitates. It might even be said to tyrannise.

When dealing with any change, look at what is pushing you towards the change and also what is pulling you away from it. Focus on each decision, one at a time and in priority order.

8. Be excited by change and what could be

Change can generate infinite possibilities and growth. Reframe the situation by being excited and lose the words 'nervous', 'anxious' and 'overwhelmed'. Focus on your values and not your fears, and let your thoughts and actions feed into this. Think about what could go right – refer back to a positive change you have experienced before and the outcome of that. Have an open and curious mindset and you will notice things you might have missed if you had blinkers on.

Practising gratitude and identifying at least three positives per day can reinforce good things often taken for granted. It also helps you to build resilience for when things are challenging.

Now it's time to unwrap your GIFT of Change

Take some time to think about the questions below.

G Grow

- What key lessons has the gift taught you?
- In what ways has it helped you to learn and grow?

I Integrate

- How will you incorporate these lessons into your life moving forward?
- What do you need to be aware of and what could get in the way of you actioning these lessons?

F Facilitate

- What lessons from this gift can you share with others professionally or personally?
- Who will you share these with and how will you share this gift?

T Transform

- How will you know that this gift has transformed you and others?
- When will you share this gift with others?

Your Change Bomboniera

- Change is the only constant in life. It can be chosen or forced upon us. Change can be the portal to growth, possibility and new directions.
- Our 'why' to change must exceed our 'why' to stay the same. To embrace known and unknown change, we need a compelling reason and the motivation to do so.
- Tap into past skills and experiences that have got you through change before. Know what motivates and lights you up when dealing with change – this can energise you to get through.
- Change is a process; having an open mind and patience is vital. Change takes effort, so ensure you have the mindset and energy to implement the change and not take on too many changes and decisions at once.
- Look at change as an opportunity to set a new direction; the Gift of Change equates to transformation and can reinforce your purpose and strength as a person.

Thirteen

THE GIFT OF GROWTH

> *If we don't change, we don't grow. If we don't grow, we aren't really living.* —Anatole France

In this chapter, we will delve into the things that can stifle growth and the importance of stepping out of our safe zone and into our stretch zone. We will explore the key elements of growth so we can expand emotionally, intellectually and spiritually.

We will unwrap:

- the things that can stunt growth in our lives
- the six keys to growth
- the GIFT process to help you unwrap your Gift of Growth and share it.

But first, I'd like to share a story that encapsulates this gift. Marie Varrasso's experience demonstrates that when we have the courage to leave our comfort zone to welcome change, we deepen our self-awareness and growth.

Marie's story

Marie Varrasso is a supply chain executive with experience at Nike, Oxford University Press (OUP) and Officeworks.

In early 2019, Marie was working in a lucrative and prestigious role at a dream company. She had notched up a 25-year career in supply chain, coupled with expat opportunities and travel to almost every continent. Yet she knew she had more to give. She had started to question her worth and her mojo had disappeared overnight. The possibility of moving overseas wasn't feasible. So, what next?

The lead-up

Marie travelled for a year in the early '90s after finishing university. Returning to Australia during the peak recession period, she utilised her Italian language skills working for Australia's then-infant pay TV industry. Within a few years she was working for global publisher OUP, one of the world's oldest companies. Her career quickly took off in supply chain as a director, travelling around the world, living in Singapore and Oxford, England. In early 2006 she joined the 'dream' company, Nike, for a career spanning 13 years and six roles, based in its Australian head office and travelling worldwide.

Not an easy decision

Leaving Nike was the most difficult decision Marie ever had to make, but she knew it was the right move. She realised she needed to change the way she thought of herself before jumping into looking for her next job, though – and she needed to identify what must change. Deep down, she knew that despite all the world had offered her, she still had to address the issues in her head. People think she's an extrovert – loud, passionate – but, really, she'd rather curl up into a ball than have all eyes on her. So she started to work on her confidence.

Marie's idea was to connect with as many people as she could on platforms such as LinkedIn and create a network. She was a guest speaker at conferences and helped university students and mentored others she met. She loved the opportunity to give back to a community that had given her so much over 25 years. Marie was even flown to Malaysia and Singapore to speak at conferences.

Marie's key learnings

Here are the standout learnings that contributed to Marie's growth, and that of others:

- **Stop and smell the roses:** Taking deep breaths helped focus and reset Marie's mind and soul. To grow as a person, you need to make the space to reflect on what you have and celebrate this. Self-reflection opens up the space for growth.
- **Connect with family and friends:** After she left Nike, Marie enjoyed lunch with the stay-at-home mums who were her childhood friends, reconnecting with herself in the process of reconnecting with them. Connection with others and ourselves is pivotal to change or self-growth.
- **Give back:** Mentoring and sharing knowledge at conferences, universities, associations and businesses taught Marie to truly listen and connect with the audience. She found that she also grew in the process. Sharing skills and life lessons with others reinforces how far we have come and how much more we can grow through contribution.
- **Network outside your comfort zone:** LinkedIn changed everything for Marie. She gained confidence by reaching out to strangers, and contributing through posts and sharing her learnings. The requests for connection kept coming. Initially Marie thought there was nothing these networkers could gain from her – after all, she was unemployed at the time. Somehow, though, what she shared resonated with many people.

- **Learn and educate yourself:** During her time out of work, Marie learned about leadership, the future of supply chain and the consumer. She read countless books and articles, and connected with the big four consultancy firms which, in turn, invited her to their seminars and luncheons. It helped Marie plan a strategy for her next career move.
- **Be open and explore new opportunities:** By looking harder and deeper at opportunities, Marie met many people who changed her life. Breaking out of her safe and comfortable zone by sharing and giving back to others enabled growth.

As you can see, Marie had to embrace the unknown in order to grow and thus change her trajectory. Being highly self-aware and accepting the changes she needed to embrace, she experienced real growth to be able to adopt the Gift Mindset and share her story.

Be brave for growth

Today, Marie works at Officeworks, travels domestically weekly, and is happy making a difference to 500-plus team members. She believes if you want to grow, you need to think about making brave changes in your life.

Growth comes when we put ourselves out there and live outside our comfort zone. Whether growth is forced upon us or is a conscious decision, as it was for Marie, there is nothing to lose and much more to gain. Take it as an opportunity to sharpen the saw and become your fuller self. The Gift of Growth is a continuous one and we need to push ourselves to be open to it.

What can stunt growth?

Many factors can stifle growth in all areas of our lives. What has the potential to become a full-grown oak tree can end up a bonsai if we're not aware of what could hold us back. Many things that can stunt growth exist subconsciously; therefore, reflection, awareness and action are key.

Invest in the time to identify what could be holding back growth for you right now, or what may be holding back growth lessons from your past. In my experience, I've found the following to be the most likely growth stunters:

- procrastination
- lack of goals or direction
- being out of touch with our emotional or spiritual side
- allowing fear to drive decisions
- lack of time (real or perceived)
- low emotional intelligence
- not taking responsibility
- lack of courage
- lack of self-discipline
- lack of awareness of growth opportunities
- anxiety and fear
- lack of motivation
- pride
- complacency or laziness.

Get comfortable being uncomfortable

I believe pushing ourselves outside our safe zone triggers learning by expanding our thinking. Growth is anything outside what we think we know – being stretched outside what you know helps you discover new ways to do (and not do) things.

Taking risks and challenging the status quo can set the scene for others to follow and adopt a 'comfortable being uncomfortable' mindset. With change as the only constant, stretching ourselves and others is key to staying relevant, challenged and innovative in today's business landscape. Doing everyday things differently ensures you will continue to step outside your safe zone, in and out of the workplace.

Think of the rings in a cross-section of timber, where each ring represents a zone. As we get used to being in a zone it becomes safe and comfortable – we need to stretch ourselves and break through to the next zone. Each breakthrough equals growth.

Question how things are done and share new ideas – this can take you and others outside your comfort zone.

Using the below model, reflect on where you sit on the comfort/ growth scale. You will notice that high growth comes from getting uncomfortable and stretching yourself out of your safe zone.

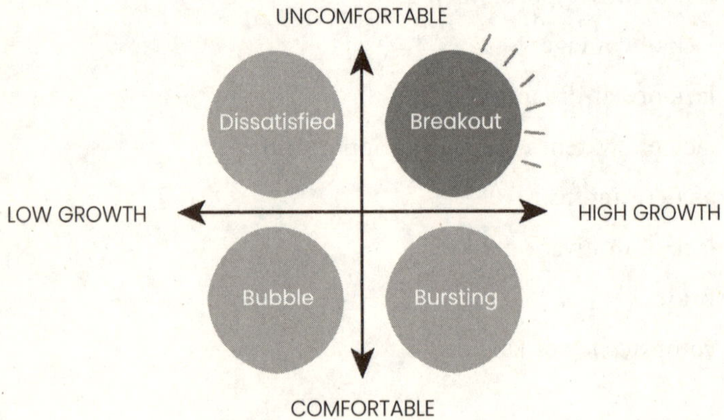

Growth as a leader

In any position, but especially a leadership position, growth is vital in order to create future leaders, share knowledge and experience and foster a learning environment.

My business conducted a Limitless Leaders™ survey across hundreds of our clients. We asked people to rate a series of statements with the following choice of responses:

- Exactly like me
- A lot like me
- Somewhat like me
- A little like me
- Not at all like me

Here are a few key findings from the survey in relation to growth:

Statement	Result
I evolve, learn and unlearn in order to grow myself.	75% responded 'exactly like me'
I get excited learning new things.	91% responded 'exactly like me'
I open myself up to growing and being more as a leader.	43% responded 'exactly like me'; 34% responded 'a lot like me'
I think it's possible to grow, learn and evolve as a leader.	63% responded 'exactly like me'; 28% responded 'a lot like me'

The results from the survey were refreshing. Growth is a core human need and we must embrace opportunities to grow – and review and renew habits around self-growth – to ensure we make the space.

> *Real change can happen by focusing on being 1% better each day, as all habits are the compound interest of self-improvement.* —James Clear

Triggers of growth

Many factors trigger growth – these can come from within us or from outside. Facing a crisis, learning something new, going through change or upskilling in a particular area – these are a combination of external and internal triggers. A growth mindset, or what I call a bursting mindset – where you believe your abilities are fluid and changeable – focuses on learning more skills and honing our talents.

> *It doesn't take a great genius to recognize that when you are pushed by circumstance to do the one thing you have always most specifically loathed and feared, this can be, at the very least, an interesting growth opportunity.* —Elizabeth Gilbert

We need to tap into the Gift of Growth regularly. Looking at both the successes and challenges we have faced, whether in relationships or situations, can contribute to our growth. Past, hidden, present or future gifts of growth can accumulate to provide a solid platform for future growth.

Remember, growth can be emotional, intellectual and spiritual, and as humans we have a constant need for development across all three areas.

The six keys to growth

Let's now take a look at the six keys to continual growth.

1. Embrace change and challenge yourself

When faced with chosen or forced change, be open to embracing it. Understanding the reason and payoff for the change can motivate you. Change forces us to grow, and our biggest challenges usually provide the biggest opportunities for growth. Look at ways of getting out of your comfort zone, and be open to the unknown and what could be.

2. Reframe struggles as growth opportunities

Reframing, sometimes referred to as cognitive reframing, is a technique to help create a different way of looking at a situation, person, idea or relationship by changing its meaning. This creates a different perspective. An example is reframing the word 'challenge' to 'opportunity'. This simple reframe can enable you to focus on what you *can* do, rather than just seeing a situation as negative or hard. Another example is reframing a thought such as *This is such a scary experience* to *This experience is exciting; I could learn so much.*

3. Adopt a bursting mindset

By believing you can grow and continue to improve yourself, you become receptive to more growth. A bursting mindset is open to change – things that are new and different – and holds a belief that things aren't fixed. Align your priorities with your values and goals by making sure that what you are looking to grow is relevant to your needs and direction. How will it serve you, your home team and your work team? Be open to emotional, spiritual and intellectual growth. Remember, when we experience growth, we have more to contribute to others and this, in turn, helps us and those around us to grow.

4. Live in the present

Your past can teach you lessons that can be applied now and your future can open possibility and progress. However, learning and growing in the now is essential. We create what happens to us. Think about your growth priorities right now and what you can action. Our future is the result of our thoughts, feelings and actions in the now.

5. Get a coach or mentor

Find someone who will challenge and help drive your growth; someone honest who is invested in your success. International Coaching Federation studies showed that 70% of executives receiving regular coaching improved their work performance, and 72% said it impacted their communication skills positively. You may have an informal or formal relationship with your mentor or coach – they could be a work colleague, a friend, a partner, an ex-boss or someone outside your existing network. Be open to collaborating on your success with someone who fits with your needs, and change mentors and coaches regularly to gain new insights and learnings.

6. Make self-growth a priority

Never stop learning and educating yourself. Self-growth starts with self-discipline, and a great way to do this is to create new habits around your growth. For example, reading not only increases your knowledge base but it also helps you learn new words, create new thoughts and ideas, and grows your brain and memory function. Knowledge is power and sharing what you learn can evoke thought and conversation in others.

We all have a preferred learning style, be it visual, physical or aural. Know what works for you, so you can be as receptive as possible to learning. Read books, listen to podcasts, study, attend webinars, contribute on social media, attend meet-ups and go to association events. Choose what works for you and make sure whatever you are learning is relevant to your growth. Self-growth can take place on the job or simply by going through changes and being open to the lessons.

My mum's gift

My amazing mother went through a time of huge growth at a young age. She married my dad in the late '60s at age 18. He was Italian and at this time it was forbidden, and unheard of, to marry someone from a different culture. She then lost both her parents, faced the devastation of losing a child, and when she divorced my father she had three children under the age of 10 to look after. She personifies the Gift of Growth to me. The lessons she experienced have enabled her to get through many challenges in life, and she has taught my sister, brother and me how important growth and change can be.

Mum got her strength from accepting the challenges she faced and embracing them, as opposed to resisting them. She says it helped having a strong purpose – to look after us kids, make us happy and shelter us as much as she could from everything. She became resilient, with no choice but to learn to cope and stay focused on progress. Empathy helped her deal with my dad almost losing his family when they married, and hearing this made me realise how all of the 12 Gifts in this book are integrated.

My mum believes her growth came from having to move forward knowing that every choice she made would impact on many things, and so she had to embrace the process. Many things she faced were devastating, yet she said she knew some of them would lead to happiness further down the track.

She always said I should ask myself this question at the end of each day:

> *What was the best thing that happened today, and what is something I have learned?*

I always reflect on this question, and not a day goes by that I haven't learnt something new or found gratitude in something I could have easily taken for granted, no matter how large or small. It could be a new way to do (or not do) something, an insight from someone else or a new way of thinking about a situation or person.

Growth is all around us. We need to be open and aware, and welcome the unwelcome at times. We also need to look at ways to deliberately create growth within us and others, for the right reasons.

Now it's time to unwrap your GIFT of Growth

Take some time to think about the questions below.

G Grow

- What key lessons has the gift taught you?
- In what ways has it helped you to learn and grow?

I Integrate

- How will you incorporate these lessons into your life moving forward?
- What do you need to be aware of and what could get in the way of you actioning these lessons?

F Facilitate

- What lessons from this gift can you share with others professionally or personally?
- Who will you share these with and how will you share this gift?

T Transform

- How will you know that this gift has transformed you and others?
- When will you share this gift with others?

Your Growth Bomboniera

- Growth is a human need linked to contribution. When we grow, we can share what we have learnt and grow others. This in turn promotes further growth within us.
- We can grow intellectually, spiritually and emotionally by going through change, embracing challenges and putting in place deliberate self-growth practices.
- Embracing change and reframing our thoughts around challenging situations and people can help us be more open to growth. Adopting a bursting mindset can create a platform for growth.
- Bring in lessons from the past, but remember that what you do, think and be today will contribute to who you become in the future. Engage in a mentoring and coaching relationship with someone who will challenge you.
- Create habits around ways to contribute to your self-growth – create a reading habit, listen to podcasts, attend association events, study, and give and get value on social media platforms.

Fourteen

THE GIFT OF CONNECTION

Invisible threads are the strongest ties. —Friedrich Nietzsche

Connection is an innate human need; we are all wired to connect. We need to make the time to connect with ourselves and others, both in and out of the workplace. This builds and strengthens deep relationships and interactions, much needed in the busyness of the world today.

As we explore the Gift of Connection, we will unwrap:

- the five ways to connect as a leader
- easy connection hacks
- the drivers of whole connection
- the 11 keys to connection
- the GIFT process to unwrap your Gift of Connection and share it.

First, I'd like to reflect on the way today's instantaneous access has changed connection.

Streaming, not teaming

In mid-2019, the last remaining Blockbuster Video store in Australia shut its doors. This got me thinking about how we used to have those amazing experiences where we would go into the store, choose a video to watch, and plan when we were going to watch it. We had to make sure we had it back on the due date (I was never good at that) so we didn't incur a late fee. These days, this experience is a distant memory; what we have instead is streaming. At any time, we can instantly stream a movie via Apple, Netflix, Foxtel or Stan, watch it when we want, pause it when we want and, sometimes, even choose our own endings.

It's a bit like conversations, connections and interactions in life. Our expectation of instantaneous access has made us more impulsive and much less intentional. This is affecting the way we connect with ourselves and those around us.

To me, it seems we are all having what I call 'streaming conversations' – conversations that are very topical, high level, and don't really cut through to the personal level. There seems to be very little of what I call 'teaming conversations' – conversations that connect us at a deep level, are intentional and transformational, and help us to build deeper relationships.

For example, I recently observed a leader talking to his team in an open-plan office. He was perched over their desks, casually congratulating them on achieving the highest engagement survey result in the business. This was a pretty big achievement and it deserved to be celebrated. However, not all members of the team were engaged in the conversation; the buzz of the office was loud and distracting, and the leader's message was rushed, impulsive and ultimately missed its mark. This is typical of a 'streaming conversation'. Although I'm sure the leader had good intentions, he should have made the time to get the team together in an appropriate space so that everyone was present and engaged. This would have ensured greater buy-in, and provided a forum for structured conversation, input from the team and dedicated time to go deeper. Overall, the message would have been more intentional, the discussion and engagement deeper and the interaction more memorable and well received.

Connecting at a deeper level

Connection is about being associated with someone or something. Scientific research shows that human connection makes us healthier, happier and more productive.

During the 2020 global pandemic, when most of us were physically disconnected, we found ways to connect virtually with our teams, loved ones and friends. The conduit to connection changed from face to face to virtual (utilising technology such as Zoom), but the yearning for connection at a deep, human level never ceased. If anything, I observed an increase in the need and want for connection between my clients and the teams and businesses they were leading.

By sharing our stories, lessons and experiences with others we can connect at a deeper level. I call this being an 'essence' connector. This is the opposite of being a 'topical' connector, where you engage in many conversations and interactions of the streaming type, as outlined earlier.

If you're a topical connector, you may rely on social media, text messages and top-line impulsive interactions to keep your connections afloat. A topical interaction could start with 'How are you?', a default question many of us ask. The response is normally something like 'Not bad' or 'All good', then the person asking directs the conversation towards what they want to talk about. In contrast, when we practise 'essence connection', we are more intentional and thoughtful with our questions. We might ask, 'What is the best thing that has happened for you today?' and give the other person space to share on a deeper level. Essence connection is like a slow-cooked meal – cooked with love, as opposed to being quickly whipped up and served in a rush.

When we connect more deeply we are open to sharing and adopting the Gift Mindset, both in and out of the workplace. This can lead to more intentional interactions that can result in meaningful, connective relationships.

By connecting deeply and valuing our interactions, we can build rapport and influence as a leader and in life. To do this, we need to take the time to meaningfully tap into ourselves, our relationships and the situations we encounter. Most importantly, we need to connect with ourselves and build our emotional intelligence to connect effectively with others. Psychologist Daniel Goldman says we need to understand our own emotions and trigger points in order to manage them; this, in turn, helps us manage and understand others' trigger points and emotions.

Connection comes down to proactively forging and tapping into situations where connection is possible. Evidence shows that people who are isolated or feel chronically lonely are up to 10 times more likely to die prematurely than people with strong connections to other people. And, as Dale Carnegie said, you can make more friends in two months by becoming interested in other people than you can in two years by trying to get other people to be interested in you.

We have never been more exposed to technology and faster ways to do things, but we've also never been more disconnected. Distraction and clutter are high in our lives, and we need to cut through them to establish real, meaningful connections.

> *As connected as we are with technology, it's also removed us from having to have human connection and it's made it more convenient to not be intimate.* —Sandra Bullock

Connection can be seen, it can be felt; sometimes you can almost taste it. Chris, a sales manager and client of mine in the building and construction industry, has such a connected team that when you walk into his office, you feel it. Everyone is happy, and that has a flow-on effect: the team's staff retention is amazing, and it's one of the highest-performing areas in the company.

Ensure you are connecting with the human side, and not just defaulting to technology. Steve Jobs created devices for connection because he had trouble connecting with people in real life. He invented the iPhone because it could create a rich creative process and assist people like him to form connections.

Connect with yourself to connect with others

In my early 20s I left the cocoon of Melbourne, where I'd grown up, and took off to be a summer camp counsellor and dance teacher in Connecticut, the US.

I knew nobody. Although surrounded by hundreds of people at Camp America, I felt lonely. I missed my friends and my family. Connection through letters – this was prior to email – kept me going. But being away from everything and everyone I knew taught me to connect with myself. It taught me how strong and independent I was. It helped me adopt a limitless mindset – I knew I could do anything if I set my mind to it.

You might not take off and do a work stint overseas, but take the time to spend some time alone, to tap into who you are. You can't connect with others unless you're connected with yourself.

Connecting with ourselves means we have to take ourselves out of our safe zone. It comes back to awareness, being present, and leaning into who we are to be in tune with our emotions, our spirituality and our physical needs.

> *It's not the mountain that we conquer, but ourselves.*
>
> —Sir Edmund Hillary

Wired to be social

Brain imaging has shown that our brains are wired to be social. If we want to build good relationships, we need to understand how to tap into the 'social brain' network, and this can help us build better connectivity between individuals. It's not just about remembering what people told you, taking notes or remembering names – the key is perception. Because we're wired to be social, we look for social cues – things we see in real time that can display connection.

There are many ways we can connect. The coordination of our brain and heart can be sparked by what we hear and see. For example, a technique known as mirroring is where two people's body language is in sync – this subconsciously increases emotional engagement.

> *I define connection as the energy that exists between people when they feel seen, heard, and valued; when they can give and receive without judgment.* —Brené Brown

Building rapport at a deep level is part of connection. When you hear people say, 'We just clicked', that is rapport. Whether you're leading a team, or interacting with clients or friends, it is cues such as finishing each other's sentences, sitting the same way, even coming up with the same wording that let you know you're building connection. When you're communicating on a deep level with another person, you see things from their vantage point.

Think about the Gift of Connection, and one of your connections that may be weak. How can you ramp that up?

Connection is vital – take the time to be present and go deep with others. Build rapport and connect because connection isn't just a preferred trait – we are *wired* to connect.

Connecting as a leader

People in a position of leadership need to connect deeply to gain trust, rapport, influence and buy-in. When a conductor leads an orchestra, trust, rapport and connection must be present for the performance to be of a high standard. These are *people* skills rather than *technical* skills. Leading people requires a focus on people before process and progress. Failing to connect is failing to lead.

Leaders also need to be open, honest and bold and provide feedback in real time, even if it causes disconnection; for example, when delivering constructive or confronting feedback. I believe a workplace culture strong in feedback and gratitude will always trump a transactional performance-based culture.

> *Connect, create meaning, make a difference, matter, be missed.*
> —Seth Godin

According to Seth Godin:

> *When someone tells you what you need to hear, instead of what you're hoping to hear, you've found something priceless. When you offer this gift to someone else, it might seem like it's unappreciated. But you didn't do it to be appreciated, you did it because you care enough to work for a deep connection.*

This quote reinforces that we need to be intentional and authentic in the way in which we connect. By doing this our interactions and relationships are more meaningful.

Here are my top five ways to connect as a leader:

1. Coach by asking questions to empower others to think for themselves. Take the time to let the other person respond – draw out information so that you get to understand them more. Be present and in the moment to connect at a deeper level.

2. Use technology to complement human connection, not replace it. Don't overuse virtual conferencing; instead, mix up the ways in which you connect and find out your team members' preferences.

3. Mix it up with a walk-and-talk meeting. Don't always sit in your office – get out into neutral territory. Walking with my one-on-one clients during coaching I often have to ask them to slow down, but we're still in rapport because we're side by side, and they begin to open up a lot more. It's a great way to get some exercise, too.
4. Have lunch with your team. Ask each person to bring something to eat, and enjoy this time together. The whole ritual of eating and sharing together goes back to ancient times – food is connection.
5. Eliminate technology when you're connecting face to face. Have phones out of sight or away from the lunch table and laptops down – these form a barrier. By being in the moment, you'll save time and connect at a deeper level.

Connecting with your customers

An anecdote in *Forbes* tells of a customer ringing Zappos' customer-care centre to return some boots that she had bought for her father, who had died. They responded saying not to worry about returning them. They would refund her money and she could give the boots away instead. After the call, they sent her some flowers – one of 380 gifts of flowers they sent to customers that year.

Encouraging phone calls 24/7 enables Zappos' employees to have deep conversations with their customers, helping them build social connection. Soft skills, or 'life skills', are crucial to form relationships, and are the only way to engage at a human level and build trust.

Focus on commonalities

A great way to connect and build rapport is to maximise similarities – commonalities – and minimise differences.

When working with clients, I've noticed that the businesses where people tend to focus on their differences are usually the ones with people whining at the water cooler – not a great use of time.

You can find commonalities with anyone – whether you've both got a dog or children, or even just share the same workplace. Sharing these commonalities is powerful. It helps people work together and motivate each other, and drives collaboration and connection in and out of the workplace.

In one study, scientists scanned the brains of monkeys that hadn't had much social interaction to measure how they worked with connection. These monkeys were placed in different groups – one monkey with one other monkey, another with two monkeys, another with seven monkeys and another in a bigger group of 20 monkeys. They lived in these groups for a few months, then the scientists scanned the monkeys' brains again. They found that the brains of the monkeys that were in the larger-size groups had grown significantly larger than those of the monkeys from the smaller groups. This experiment demonstrated that having to connect and be in an environment with other monkeys helps develop what is known as the 'social brain muscle'.

Tell stories

As we learned in chapter 5, stories go back to ancient times. They evoke emotion and thought, and can bind us together – no matter who we are, where we're from; whether we're rich or poor, young or old. Research shows that people are more likely to remember a story than hard data and statistics.

Growing up, I vividly remember sitting around the dinner table or a campfire hearing other people's stories. My dad used to captivate my sister and me by weaving the amazing adventures of Leroy the Worm into our bedtime routine.

We are all storytellers. We all live in a network of stories. There isn't a stronger connection between people than storytelling.
—Jimmy Neil Smith, Founder, International Storytelling Center

No matter who you are, you're a storyteller. We've all been telling stories since we were children, from the playground and 'show and tell' at school, to at home with our families. Incorporating stories to connect in the business world or in your personal life – it's all the same thing. Sharing your stories effectively is powerful.

Stories can motivate; they can connect us no matter where we're from. My favourite teacher, Mr Fry, taught us in primary school through storytelling – the year he taught me stands out the most.

Human connections are deeply nurtured in the field of storytelling. —Jean Houston

To connect in today's world, tap into storytelling. Companies and people all over the world share their stories via text, video, images and photos. Storytelling has always been there, but it's more important than ever to avoid the disconnect of non-physical interactions. Share a story to connect face to face or on social media platforms such as Facebook, YouTube, Instagram and LinkedIn.

To share a story, tell it with your heart, your mind and with feeling. Keep a journal of all the interesting things you experience; practise storytelling with your friends and with your team; and make a conscious effort to bring storytelling into your leadership and into your life.

Here are my three tips for great storytelling:

1. Share the experience – be real, be raw.
2. Share the values that were involved in that story.
3. Share the success or the failure, and the lessons others can benefit from.

Sharing a story is what the Gift Mindset is all about. The Gift of Connection is a powerful channel to do this.

The drivers of whole connection

The four parts of whole connection mean being connected to both yourself and those around you.

We must have deep connections with ourselves before we can forge and grow meaningful relationships with others. Let's take a look at how the four parts of whole connection work.

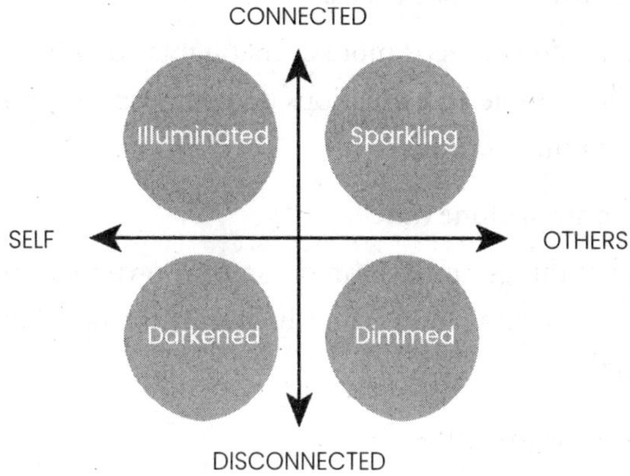

1. Darkened – disconnected from self

If you're in this space you may lack self-reflection, be time-poor, have low self-awareness or be drawing on past experiences that are holding you back. These are just some of the factors that may contribute to us being disconnected from ourselves.

Here are some clear signs that you are living in the 'darkened' space:

- your progress is on hold
- your thoughts and emotions are negative
- your health is suffering
- you numb out to avoid dealing with things
- you tend to avoid social interaction.

As with any relationship, building a relationship with yourself can take time and you need to be patient, open and focused. Here are five ways I have found to build a deeper self-connection:

1. **Take the time to be self-aware.**
   - Notice and accept your thoughts, feelings and actions.
   - Lock in a time every day to notice these and journal them.
2. **Pay attention to your needs.**
   - What do you need more of that lights you up?
   - What people and situations do you need to eliminate or bring into your life?
3. **Give yourself alone time.**
   - What things can you can do on your own that bring you joy?
   - Try new things and jealously protect the time you need to do these.
4. **Know your strengths.**
   - Remind yourself of your skills, strengths and capabilities.
   - Reinforce where your strengths lie and use these.
5. **Have self-compassion.**

   Use the CAN process (outlined in chapter 5):
   - **C – Confess:** To the pain or event; what is happening?
   - **A – Align:** To others who may feel this; who else is experiencing this?
   - **N – Nourish:** Yourself; what can you do or think that will help you?

2. Dimmed – disconnected from others

Being 'dimmed' and disconnected from others can be linked to low self-connection. It may cause us to avoid connection with others and this can sometimes occur at a subconscious level and can be at the cost of our health, relationships and growth.

In our personal lives we need deep connection for support, learning and growth – and this is mirrored in the workplace. Your network in and outside your industry mirrors your connection with yourself and others. The people involved and the levels of connection will change continuously, but it's important to invest time in maintaining those relationships.

Connection with others needs to be a priority in order to grow and, in the process, feel deeply fulfilled and happy. I've come across people who've been disconnected from others due to poor health, trauma and even just busyness. This can prevent happiness and healing, among other things.

In the workplace, many can become overwhelmed at the breadth of potential connections, and therefore retreat into themselves. British anthropologist Professor Robin Dunbar and other researchers have found we only have the emotional bandwidth for a certain number of people in our network. The magic number is 150. The research is based on a ratio between brain sizes and group sizes, and the ability to invest enough energy and time to develop deep relationships and form kinships – not just friendships.

The Rule of 150 is defined as the:

> *suggested cognitive limit to the number of people with whom one can maintain stable social relationships and thus numbers larger than this generally require more restrictive rules, laws, and enforced norms.*

Kinship is a type of connection that rarely decays due to time or geographical distance. Reflecting on kinship, I think of people I may not see often, but our bond is so strong that we always have a deep connection when we do get in touch. These are the people you could ask a favour from at any time, and vice versa, no matter how long it has been since you saw each other.

The number of 150 was as true for early hunter-gatherer societies as it is for modern offices, communes, residential campsites and military organisations – even a Christmas-card list.

Attention is the equivalent to oxygen in building relationships.

If we exceed the magic number, it is unlikely that all the relationships in our network will last long or cohere well. The key barriers include the cognitive challenge of keeping track of more than 150 people, as well as the time to build and maintain these relationships. Friendships and relationships require emotion, and Dunbar believes touch is more powerful than words – something we cannot access virtually on social networks. Many of us have thousands of followers on social media platforms; however, these so-called connections are rarely in the physical form.

Dunbar's Number

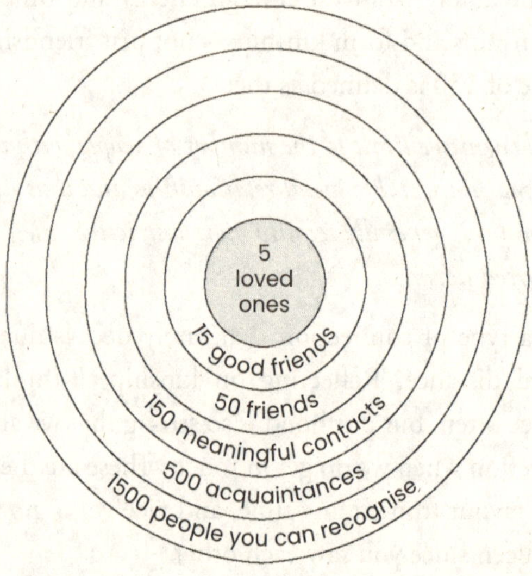

Source: Adapted from R Dunbar (2010), *How Many Friends Does One Person Need?: Dunbar's Number and Other Evolutionary Quirks*, Faber.

Let's take a look at my top six ways to build a deeper connection with others:

1. **Apply Dunbar's model.**
   - List in order: 5 loved ones, 15 good friends, 50 friends, 150 meaningful contacts.
   - Review the list and eliminate and augment.
2. **Communicate.**
   - Be clear, honest and concise.
   - Listen deeply and be present.
   - Be intentional in what you share.
   - Ensure the message is understood.
3. **Lock in personal time with people.**
   - Connect over food or a common interest.
   - Nurture these relationships.
   - Be mutually invested in the relationship.
4. **Build rapport.**
   - Take the time for small talk.
   - Listen to what is *not* being said.
   - Show interest in others and the value you can give, not just receive.
   - Use someone's name often.
5. **Have a curious mindset.**
   - Ask questions.
   - Pay attention and be genuine.
   - Be open to not knowing everything.
6. **Network.**
   - Build a strategic plan to network.
   - List those you could give value to, get value from, and connect with.
   - Attend relevant events: meet-ups, industry associations, sporting clubs.

3. Sparkling – connected with others

If you are 'sparkling', you are deeply connected with yourself and with people in all areas of your life. You have much to share with others.

Our connections with others shape our values, our boundaries and even our identity. Who I am has a lot to do with all the experiences I've had, both with and through others. Many things I'm currently doing have resulted from connections – some people are still in my life; a few I crossed paths with for a season.

Connections lead to connections – you may be time-poor, but make sure you make the time to connect deeply. If you are 'sparkling', share your gift with others, and maintain and grow it.

Here are four signs you're in the 'sparkling' zone:

1. You have deep and meaningful relationships, both in and out of the workplace. You value the importance of these relationships.
2. You feel lit up, motivated and enthusiastic to interact. Connections energise you.
3. Your values and energy are aligned. You give and get value from relationships and you communicate openly.
4. Your relationships mutually support and serve personal growth. Vulnerability and disclosure are present, as is the openness to challenge each other.

Keep in mind that our connections can change, and we need to remain aware of who we are in service to and who serves us. I invest in the time to be around those who light me up, challenge me and support me, as I do in turn for them.

Recently I worked with Rick, a marketing director who was struggling to build deeper relationships across the different business units in his team. We sat down and explored who he was networking with. He tended to spend his time building deep relationships with certain people, but not people outside his team. We looked at who he could add value to and get value from and scoped out a plan of action. Rick invested in the time to be intentional in broadening and deepening his relationships, which has since opened many doors for him and his team and, above all, has skyrocketed his growth and continued progress.

Strategic networking is crucial at work. Humans tend to connect with people we like and who are easy to connect with, yet sometimes the people we need to connect with are the more difficult people. If you're 'sparkling', you're taking the time to connect with a wide range of different personalities, both in and out of the workplace.

4. Illuminated – deep self-connection

When you are 'illuminated', you have high self-awareness. You are in touch with your capabilities and shortcomings, and the opportunities that surround you. You know your strengths and what lights you up – you tap into this as much as possible.

People who have deep self-connection find it empowering to spend time alone – it is a part of their routine. They have high self-compassion – they are kind to themselves and can easily direct love inwards.

We are wired for survival and empathy. Did you know we have mirror neurons in our brains that fire when we see people's pain? Being connected can assist us to break down the walls containing our potential to live our authentic selves, and thus make the contribution we were born to make.

For us to accept our gifts, we need to open the door and invite self-compassion into our lives. The more connected we are to ourselves, the more connected we will be with others.

The 11 keys to connection

Here are my 11 keys to deepen your connections with colleagues, loved ones and yourself.

1. ***Be present.***
2. ***Build rapport.***
3. ***Communicate openly.***
4. ***Show empathy.***
5. ***Have compassion for self and others.***
6. ***Have a curious mindset.***
7. ***Reinforce positives.***
8. ***Master your social skills.***
9. ***Show appreciation.***
10. ***Adopt a Gift Mindset.***
11. ***Share a story to connect.***

Now it's time to unwrap your GIFT of Connection

Take some time to think about the questions below.

G Grow

- What key lessons has the gift taught you?
- In what ways has it helped you to learn and grow?

I Integrate

- How will you incorporate these lessons into your life moving forward?
- What do you need to be aware of and what could get in the way of you actioning these lessons?

F Facilitate

- What lessons from this gift can you share with others professionally or personally?
- Who will you share these with and how will you share this gift?

T Transform

- How will you know that this gift has transformed you and others?
- When will you share this gift with others?

Your Connection Bomboniera

- We are all wired to connect. Our connection with others can shape our values, boundaries and parts of our identity.
- It's imperative to have deep self-connection in order to connect with others. Make it a priority to create awareness around this and practise habits to build self-connection.
- Clear, concise and open communication is key. Be honest and present and listen deeply. Build rapport by being a bit more like the other person.
- Aim for 150 connections in order to forge, develop and sustain deep relationships. This can include personal and professional connections.
- Adopt a curious mindset by asking questions, paying attention and being open to learning about others.

Fifteen

THE GIFT OF EMPATHY

> *Empathy is seeing with the eyes of another, listening with the ears of another and feeling with the heart of another.*
> —Alfred Adler

Expressing and receiving empathy is vital in any role, interaction and relationship. Living the Gift of Empathy throughout our lives helps us to live from a place of understanding, care and empathetic connection.

As we explore the Gift of Empathy we will unwrap:

- the six keys to empathy
- empathy versus sympathy
- the three layers of empathy
- the GIFT process to unwrap your Gift of Empathy and share it.

First, I'd like to share a story from Claudio Conte, Founder of Spiral Orb Designs. He tells of an incident where words changed everything for him.

Claudio's story

'I launched my first business at 23 years old,' he says. 'FIT 4 U was a health and fitness business inside Alterego Holistic Fitness Studio, owned by Hamish Cramer. I was making just enough to cover my rent for the space by working part-time as a bartender on weekends.

'One Saturday morning, tired and wanting to get home quickly, I was taking rural roads home from a bar and doing close to 130km/h in a 100km/h zone. I was pulled over, my licence was suspended and I was sent to court. I tried negotiating with the judge to drop my one-month suspension, as my business meant everything to me and I was on the verge of letting go of life if I couldn't make it work. I remember her saying, "Are you really trying to negotiate with me here?", but she gave me a week off my suspension. A sign of empathy, perhaps?

'That's it, I thought. Even though I negotiated, it felt like fighting a battle knowing I'd already lost.'

Words changed everything

'The next week I went into the studio to tell Hamish that it was over – I wouldn't be able to get to the gym while my licence was suspended. That was when the magic unfolded. He asked, "What could you do to make it work for the next three weeks?" Thinking about it, I noticed the couch in the office. "I could sleep here," I said. "If we had a mini fridge, I could walk 20 minutes down to the shops to get food."

'Hamish organised the mini fridge. It wasn't an easy three weeks, but I did it and about a month on from this experience my business exploded. I left my bartender job, and soon became the busiest trainer at the gym. I learned that absolutely nothing could stop me.'

The gift

'Hamish will probably never know how much his act meant. It allowed me to grow, learn more about myself and the world, and that business could mean meeting incredible people and, in the process, changing hundreds of lives.

'I gave my loyalty to Hamish and he showed me what I was capable of. The empathy he displayed has led me to have many more growth encounters. I opened a new company, and now lead my own team and collaborate with incredible human beings, tapping into my own empathy towards my staff, clients and partners.

'So how do I apply empathy in my leadership now? I listen intently to what my team and clients are asking for, detaching where possible from my business outcomes and focusing on the people.

'I find that when my team or clients ask or give feedback, I can be present and support them in ways that I wouldn't previously have been aware of. I have learnt that if you give without an expectation of return, you open the door to empathy. This translates in turn into more loyalty, more business and a reputation I am proud of.'

The importance of empathy

Empathy has the ability to connect you to deeper parts of yourself, which in turn results in drastic changes in your environment and outcomes. It can help attract the right people who are willing to be led by you and to work alongside you.

All you need is the awareness to see what is happening in front of you; to set aside beliefs, ego and fear.

We know that tapping into human connection gives us the best results, not only in our businesses but in our lives. Claudio's story emphasises that empathy doesn't have to be complicated or hard. It's often the simple gestures, words and decisions that create the biggest impact. Claudio's Gift of Empathy came in the form of a gift voucher from Hamish, which he could utilise as he wished.

In the workplace, it's easy to shut down when a colleague or direct report opens up to you about feeling overstretched and tired. How do you respond? Do you respond with empathy, or do you shut off, as you have your own stuff to deal with?

According to the 2018 State of Workplace Empathy study, 96% of employees consider it important for employers to demonstrate empathy, and yet 92% believe this trait is undervalued in their workplaces. Many factors prevent or stifle people from understanding and sharing emotions with their team members. Some people believe empathy is a sign of weakness – a trait they don't want to be associated with. Other factors include deadlines, stress and distractedness. These barriers to empathy can block the empathetic connection that will unlock the true capability and potential of your team.

The word 'empathy' is derived from the Greek *empatheia*, but its meaning comes from the German word *einfühlung* – literally, 'feeling in'.

Expressing the gift of empathy is vital in any role, interaction or relationship. Many people think they 'do' empathy, but how many truly 'feel in'?

Tuning in and almost physically experiencing what others may be going through gives you the greatest chance to understand others' positions and 'feel in' to what is going on. This is the way to experience true empathetic connection.

Mastering empathy as a leader and in life is a critical skill. Empathy helps create engagement and loyalty. People work better together and are happier when there is strong empathy within a team. I've found that empathy in the workplace can encourage creativity – when people feel heard and appreciated, they are more likely to take risks, share ideas and voice what they are feeling, even if it's outside the box.

Think about a time when someone really empathised with you. What did you notice and how did you feel? For me, key moments of another showing empathy stand out; although I can't articulate their words, I remember how that made me feel.

People complain when they are not feeling heard. It takes more than sympathy to make someone feel heard. The word for that 'something more' is empathy. Empathy is the most powerful change-maker in all situations, and in all relationships.

Empathy often comes naturally, but when we are under pressure we can default to not conveying it when needed. This can be subconscious, which means we are not aware that we are lacking empathy.

We need to pay attention. Attention is like oxygen to any relationship and is a key element of empathy.

Six keys to empathy

There are many ways to demonstrate and grow empathy. I have devised six keys:

1. ***Listen through their ears – be present.***
   - What are they hearing?
   - How might they interpret this?

2. ***Get in their head – pay attention to their point of view.***
   - What might they be thinking?
   - What logic might they be using to interpret the situation?

3. ***Notice their words – match with similar language.***
   - What are they saying?
   - What defining words, quotes and insights stand out?

4. View things through their eyes – imagine you are seeing what they see.

- What are they seeing?
- How does this tie into their view of the world?

5. Feel through their heart – imagine you are feeling the same thing.

- What emotions might they be feeling?
- How does this impact their actions?

6. Watch their actions – be present and pay attention.

- What are they doing?
- What actions and body language are you observing?

Empathy is about finding echoes of another person in yourself.
—Mohsin Hamid

Empathy personified

Mahatma Gandhi comes to mind as a standout empathetic leader. In 1915, on returning to India from South Africa, he decided that if he was going to campaign for Indian independence from British rule, he would need to experience what life was like for the country's poorest people. He got rid of his barrister's suit and dressed in a dhoti. He then established the Sabarmati Ashram, which became one of his residences for the next 12 years. He literally stepped into the shoes of peasant farmers during his life in the ashram, spinning his own cloth and growing the food he was to eat.

Gandhi's empathetic nature also took him across religious boundaries. Because he was appalled by the violence that existed between Muslims and Hindus, he opposed the creation of a separate Muslim state. He followed the Hindu faith, yet he famously addressed Hindu nationalists saying, 'I am a Muslim! And a Hindu, and a Christian and a Jew – and so are all of you.' These words still resonate – they stand among the greatest empathetic statements of all time. Gandhi not only spoke of empathy, but acted it.

Empathy versus sympathy

In our work educating organisations in emotional intelligence (EI) and other leadership communication skills, empathy stands out as key to building deeper relationships and connections.

I am often asked how empathy differs from sympathy.

Sympathy playing out

Recently a friend, Monique, came to me complaining about a certain person in her life. Monique needed to download and unpack the way she felt, what the other person had done to annoy her and the way this person was always letting her down. I gave her my ear and a few suggestions to deal with this person. I said, 'I can imagine what you are going through; this friend has been a big part of your life for so long.'

Monique said 'thanks for listening' but was still feeling heavy and sad, and her thoughts were still consumed by the situation. I felt sorry for her, yet at the same time my energy felt stifled.

Fast-forward three weeks: Monique downloaded again, in almost a repeat of the conversation prior. I realised nothing had changed. She hadn't actioned anything and my suggestions and words, although comforting, were only a bandaid. What I had shown was sympathy. There was no change in her energy or thoughts and I was now linked to her situation.

Empathy playing out

Recently I caught up with one of my coaching clients, Brad – a high performer who is always looking to grow. I have also worked with the leaders in his team for two years.

Brad broke down as he told me about the conflict he was having with his direct manager, who had begun to micromanage him, take credit for his ideas and even put him down for participating in external coaching. Above all, he was keeping Brad in a holding stall where he was unable to share his ideas or contribute across the broader business. Brad looked and sounded broken – even his voice lacked its usual depth. We grabbed a coffee and he talked me through all he was going through: the ins and outs, the sleepless nights, the pressure and the sick feeling he felt every morning when he woke up.

I leant into him and felt his experience. I could relate some of it to my own experience with a manager I had many years ago.

Towards the end of the conversation, I noticed that Brad's eye contact was stronger; he seemed more composed. There was a change in his overall demeanour. I also felt lighter seeing this change and that's when it hit me: my empathy and openness related to his situation and had been felt by both of us. I was feeling his experience, not just listening to it as an outsider. Brad seemed lighter and I wasn't weighed down by the conversation.

This is the pivotal difference when we demonstrate empathy over pity or sympathy.

In a nutshell, I believe sympathy makes others feel cared for and empathy makes others feel heard.

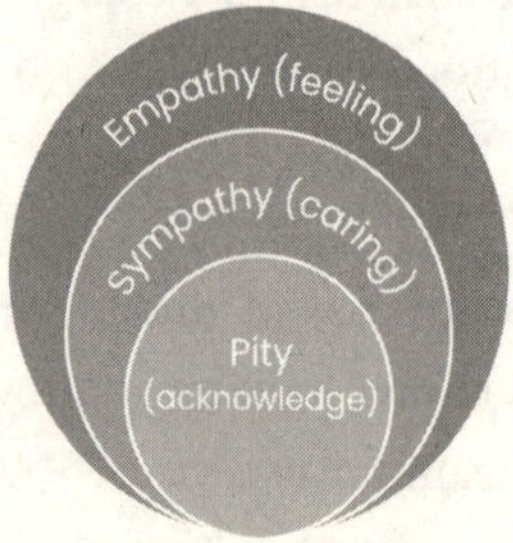

There is a place in all situations to use pity, sympathy and empathy. It will depend on the context, the person and the situation, and also your values, experiences and relationship to the topic.

When empathy is lacking

We can all recall a time when someone lacked empathy towards us or we to them. Remembering how that made you feel can be enough to ensure that you bring empathy into the way you interact in the future, helping you forge deep relationships in and out of the workplace.

As leaders, we need to include empathy as part of our everyday practice. There are enormous business costs when leaders lack the gift of empathy

One such business was United Airlines, which earned the reputation of having committed 'one of the worst corporate gaffes' in history, according to Bloomberg's Jeff Green and Christopher Palmeri, when a physician was literally dragged off his flight to give a seat to an airline employee. Not only was the incident shocking in itself, but it took United CEO Oscar Munoz three attempts before his response to the public showed any empathy.

In Munoz's first statement he said, 'I apologise for having to re-accommodate these customers.' In his second statement, Munoz compounded the error by blaming the victim – describing the passenger as defiant, belligerent and disruptive. Only with his third try, when Munoz said, 'I promise you we will do better,' did he demonstrate an empathic understanding of his current and future customers.

Lacking empathy, whatever the size of the situation, is failing to be in service to self and others, and can have ramifications that can flow into the future.

If empathy is lacking in your interactions, I suggest looking back at a time when you showed empathy. What was different? What has changed?

The three layers of empathy

Empathy is all about putting yourself in someone else's shoes – that is, seeing, feeling and experiencing what they are going through from their perspective. It's especially important if you're in a leadership position. It's not about putting others in their place.

> *Leadership is about empathy. It is about having the ability to relate to and connect with people for the purpose of inspiring and empowering their lives.* —Oprah Winfrey

Psychologists including Daniel Goleman have identified three types of empathy:

1. cognitive
2. emotional
3. compassionate.

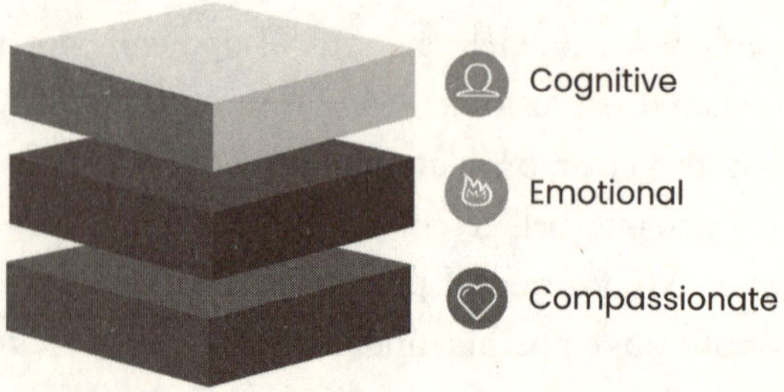

These make sense when you think about how we respond and react to what others are experiencing – in levels or layers. We also need to consider that our own level of empathy can be influenced by our mindset, experience, agenda and intention at that moment.

Let's take a look at the three layers of empathy in turn.

Cognitive empathy

This layer of empathy comes from a logical angle – *knowing* how the other person feels and what they might be thinking.

Daniel Goleman refers to this type of empathy as perspective-taking, where thought, understanding and intellect come into play. This layer of empathy is impactful when motivating others, negotiating and delving in to understand others' viewpoints.

As with anything, there are potential pitfalls. When using cognitive empathy, ensure you don't ignore or block out the deeper emotions. When *knowing* how another feels, you may not always step into *feeling* what the other person is experiencing. Be mindful of this – never assume. Ask questions and see things from the other person's perspective; learn to feel with their heart and listen through their ears.

Emotional empathy

This layer of empathy is where you *'feel into'* the other person: you feel their emotions and experience almost as if they were contagious and are now your own. Some people feel a physical response or sensation with this type of empathy.

Researchers have discovered what they call mirror neurons – a type of brain cell that responds equally when we perform an action and when we witness someone else perform it. Think of it like when you see someone whacked with a frisbee in a park (you naturally recoil in sympathy) or when watching a game of footy (your heartbeat increases as your favourite team plays to win).

Use of emotional empathy is brilliant when coaching and building close relationships. It's powerful when leading and managing. However, as with anything, it needs to be used in moderation. I naturally lean to this type of empathy and it can be overwhelming and exhausting if you don't learn to switch it off.

Compassionate empathy

With this layer of empathy, we not only *understand* a person's predicament and *feel with* them, but are spontaneously *willing to help*, if and when needed.

Intellect, emotion and action are the key ingredients. What I love about compassionate empathy is that it considers the whole person.

This type is the one we should all strive to step into as much as we can – it balances both cognitive and emotional empathy.

Did you know that feelings of the heart and thoughts of the brain are not opposites? They are in fact intricately connected. The reason compassionate empathy is so effective is that it honours that natural connection by considering both the felt senses and the intellectual situation of another person.

Remember to gauge the situation and follow your thoughts and your heart as to what type of empathy to use. I strive to use compassionate empathy as much as possible, but I also use cognitive empathy – more so when negotiating or motivating. I have been using emotional empathy of late when I've been looking after my sister, who is ill.

Now it's time to unwrap your GIFT of Empathy

Take some time to think about the questions below.

G Grow

- What key lessons has the gift taught you?
- In what ways has it helped you to learn and grow?

I Integrate

- How will you incorporate these lessons into your life moving forward?
- What do you need to be aware of and what could get in the way of you actioning these lessons?

F Facilitate

- What lessons from this gift can you share with others professionally or personally?
- Who will you share these with and how will you share this gift?

T Transform

- How will you know that this gift has transformed you and others?
- When will you share this gift with others?

Your Empathy Bomboniera

- There is a place in all situations to use pity, sympathy and empathy – depending on the context, the person, the situation and also your values, experiences and reference points.
- Pity relates to acknowledgement, sympathy relates to caring and empathy requires us to 'feel in' and make others feel heard by tuning into their experiences.
- Psychologists have identified three types of empathy: cognitive (coming from a logical angle), emotional ('feeling in' to the other person) and compassionate (considers the entire person, combining cognitive and emotional empathy).
- To demonstrate empathy, listen, take note, reflect and be open to giving and receiving empathy as part of your life.
- To 'feel in', imagine the other person's view on the world, be aware of their emotions, imagine feeling what they are going through and pay attention.

Sixteen

THE GIFT OF FORGIVENESS

Forgiveness is the fragrance that the violet sheds on the heel that has crushed it. —Mark Twain

In this chapter, we will explore the importance of forgiveness and the process and outcome of it. We will open up with an amazing story from Zamil Chowdhury where he shares insights and tips on this gift.

As we explore the Gift of Forgiveness we will unwrap:

- the benefits of forgiveness and a workplace example
- the six keys to forgiveness
- the GIFT process to help you unwrap your Gift of Forgiveness and share it.

Before we start pulling the wrapping paper off the Gift of Forgiveness, let's look at what forgiveness entails.

Psychologists define forgiveness as a deliberate and conscious decision to let go of, or release, feelings of resentment towards a person, a group or a situation. It is a process of letting go of hurt and anger, whether or not forgiveness is deserved. I think of forgiveness as an emotion and also as a verb – a process we can all access.

When we come to forgive, it doesn't mean we forget or condone what has happened. Instead, we forgive to create peace and a space to move forward. Holding onto resentment is like poison, and every human deserves peace within.

Forgiveness is rarely discussed in the workplace. Imagine, though, if you could share your Gift of Forgiveness and the lessons you gleaned? Relationships would be truer and stronger, and this could lead to a more collaborative culture.

I'd like to share a story that personifies the Gift of Forgiveness.

Zamil's story

Zamil Chowdhury has over 25 years' experience in technology. He helps organisations transform their businesses and collaborates with some of the brightest minds in the IT industry. He is passionate about the positive impact technology has on the lives of people and communities. He is an adoring father and loves to work with young people around mental health, providing mentorship through his experience, strength and hope. He lives by the mantra 'be in service to others'.

Born to a Bangladeshi father and an English-Irish mother, Zamil grew up in Birmingham, in the UK. His parents ran a café that became a hub for the local community, attracting bohemians, eclectics and the working class. It was the first time different cultures had come together in that space, and Zamil believes this was the foundation for his love of and commitment to community.

Zamil fell into his first role in IT as an assistant to the sales director. On his way through, he took the company from $100 million to $300 million; it became the largest privately owned IT company in the UK. He met his future wife and they had the ideal life, but soon burnt out and decided to travel the world. This opened their eyes to different cultures and they learned about Buddhism. Zamil started to think that there must be more to life. Following their

Vegas wedding the couple moved to Australia, but soon separated. Zamil built a community of support and was soon back working in IT.

Ten years on he met his next partner while he was working eight- to sixteen-hour days at IT company Datacom. He soon became a father and landed a huge transformational deal. All was going well until Zamil was diagnosed with cancer when his son was five. Zamil quickly became undone. Being the one orchestrating communities, he had never known where his 'off switch' was. This bought him to a standstill – he experienced denial, anger and then finally acceptance.

After nine months of chemotherapy he was relieved to be in remission. Although anxious, he defaulted back to his old ways before long. Ten months later he was re-diagnosed with cancer. During a lengthy time in hospital he contracted blood poisoning and underwent a stem cell transplant, when it was soon discovered he had a brain tumour. With all the stress of the last two years Zamil's partner, who had no family support, decided to leave the relationship. Zamil was devastated – he was questioning even being here, but any idea of ending his life soon faded as he knew he could never leave his son. Instead, Zamil immersed himself in every possible self-help resource. The cancer treatment was successful, and the brain tumour under control.

Zamil started to rebuild his life and work. He began sharing what he had learnt by mentoring and coaching young children in hospital. Around this time, out of the blue, Zamil had a stroke while at the South Melbourne Market. He recovered, but four months on he discovered his cancer had re-emerged for the third time. Before long he was in remission again. To this day Zamil credits his recovery to the self-development he had done – it was the catalyst to his healing, both inside and out.

Zamil's continual illness made him look at the dark parts of his childhood he had never faced. Up until then, he had thought that anger was the best way to deal with things. Now, Zamil realised, he was being introduced to forgiveness.

I asked Zamil how he had come to that moment of revelation. 'In order to forgive I had to have an understanding that the situation wasn't anyone's fault and I shouldn't be blaming them,' he said. He needed to take responsibility – forgiveness isn't about others but, instead, about ourselves. He realised he had been trying to control everything in his life because he didn't want to be hurt. In this moment Zamil realised what was keeping him sick: all the anger and suppressed hurt had created darkness in his body.

In Zamil's words, 'When I forgave the situation it was like shining a light into space. There was no darkness in my body whatsoever.'

With a Muslim father and a Christian mother, Zamil realised that both religions shared a focus: to love, forgive, understand and show compassion. Once he understood he had those things within him, he knew that he would be okay. Unbelievably, two days later Zamil was again diagnosed with cancer, but deep inside he knew that he was clear – with all the work he had done on forgiveness, there wasn't any space for cancer in his body. After retesting, to the doctor's shock Zamil was clear of cancer again.

Forgiveness is ...

At the core, you need to understand that there is something to forgive. You are usually holding onto some sort of resentment, anger or hurt. By acknowledging this you can seek the right support – this is vital, and no mean feat.

Zamil believes that resentment can make, and keep, us sick. Faith for him is faith in a higher power – he found the ability to lean into the discomfort of a higher power, which was paramount to his healing.

> *Forgiveness doesn't mean reconciliation or that you are justifying others' actions.*

Forgiveness is a process that will lead to what feels right for you. It requires courage, faith and understanding.

Zamil believes you need to have a framework to process forgiveness and suggests the following steps:

- **Acknowledge:** What or who do you need to forgive, and why?
- **Get support:** Tap into your resources: friends, family and, if needed, professional services. You could also tap into educational resources, religion or a spiritual path.
- **Action:** Make it happen. Do what you need to do, and be who you need to be, to let go and create peace within.

The cost of unforgiveness

Zamil's experience showed him that many negative physical, emotional and mental consequences can result from living a life of unforgiveness. Holding onto something for so long can deepen pain and prevent you from being at peace within yourself. When we are resentful and angry, we cannot lead a fulfilling life. Sometimes hitting rock bottom and reaching the point of desperation can be the catalyst – at that point, Zamil believes, the teacher or support network will show up. Take a leap of faith – this is where courage comes in and that's the beginning, wherever that takes you.

The challenge

I mentioned to Zamil that I believe that our 'why' to change must exceed our 'why' to stay the same, and this applies to forgiveness. We often need a compelling reason to pull us towards forgiveness of ourselves or others, both in and out of the workplace.

Zamil believes that he didn't deal with the hurt he endured at such a young age because he didn't know how to deal with it, and so he buried it. He says you need to be ready to deal with it, which can often depend on how much pain you will tolerate and how desperate you are.

Sometimes when we mentally revisit something shocking or unfathomable it's like walking into a bad neighbourhood on our own. We need to access the right tools, support and guidance to get through it. Sharing our experience with others who have been through a similar situation can help.

I believe many things can stifle forgiveness – both at a conscious and subconscious level – and we need to make the space so that the toxicity of unforgiveness doesn't build up and spread within us like a poison.

Zamil believes there needs to be a conversation when looking to forgive, or if you are supporting someone else in this process. You need to think about the following:

- What is the real conversation?
- How do you have the real conversation?
- How do you respond to the real conversation?

Here are Zamil's top tips for forgiveness:

- Start with self-forgiveness.
- Be brave enough to do something about forgiving others.
- Share your experience, strength and hope.
- Get the right support and connection.
- Be in service to others and support those seeking forgiveness.
- Build deep and strong relationships with those around you.
- Listen deeply to others and yourself.

As you can see from Zamil's roller-coaster experience, forgiveness does not change the past, but it does affect our future.

Forgiveness and letting go of anger have been proven to benefit a person's physical health. Studies show it lowers stress hormones, strengthens the immune system, lowers blood pressure and can reduce depression and anxiety.

I'll be the first to say it takes a lot of strength to forgive, and you need to be a strong person to be able to forgive.

Forgiveness in the workplace

Martin, a client of mine, is a national sales manager and member of his company's senior leadership team. He is great at his role: a strong leader with deep and trusting relationships within his team. Many want to emulate him to build a similar high-performance culture in their team. The company Martin works for has a strong culture of sharing best practice, including embracing the Gift Mindset by sharing learnings relating to both challenges and successes.

During an offsite strategy meeting, Martin shared some of the initiatives he and his team were working on with his fellow senior leaders. He mentioned a particular project he and his team were looking to roll out later that year with a key account customer. The idea was received positively.

Four weeks after the meeting, Martin called me in a panic. One of his peers who had been at the meeting had taken Martin's idea on board with a customer before Martin and his team had even rolled it out in their division. Martin was furious, confused and hurt.

Martin had confronted his peer and let him know his thoughts. His peer said the initiative was different from that of Martin's team, and he told Martin to chill out.

Martin and I talked through what had happened. The two teams had become distanced and Martin was now hesitant to share his ideas. This did not align with the organisational culture, which encouraged sharing and openness.

It took Martin three agonising months to get to a point where he could start to let go of the anger and resentment he was carrying. He realised it was holding him, the team and organisation back. He spoke to his peer and expressed how he felt and said that he needed to move on. His peer didn't admit fault and it took Martin time, strength and a compelling reason to forgive. He hasn't forgotten what happened; neither has his team. Further action was taken to address this from an HR perspective but all in all Martin learnt to let go for the right reasons.

Today Martin and his team are still a shining light in the organisation. His relationship with his peer is strictly professional and he continues to share best practice.

Often when we get caught up in anger and resentment, it is only us who suffer. Martin said that by really understanding his emotions and acknowledging what had happened, he was able to commit to forgiving his peer and moving on. He also has a supportive manager and network around him that he says has helped him come out the other side.

Learning to forgive ourselves and others at work, within our own family or with friends is a process that is a part of life. It takes courage and strength to forgive and the payoff is inner peace, a clear mind and a focus on moving forward.

> *Forgive others, not because they deserve forgiveness but because you deserve peace.* —Jonathan Lockwood

The benefits of forgiveness

Dr Fred Luskin, Director of the Stanford University Forgiveness Project, has completed extensive research on the training and measurement of forgiveness therapy. I was lucky enough to have a conversation with Fred.

His research demonstrates that learning forgiveness leads to increased physical vitality, hope, self-efficacy, optimism and conflict resolution skills. His research shows that forgiveness can be learned. Three separate studies were conducted, including one with Catholics and Protestants from Northern Ireland whose family members were murdered in political violence. The studies found that people who are taught how to forgive become less angry and hostile, feel less hurt and are more optimistic. They become more forgiving in a variety of situations and became more compassionate and self-confident. Fred believes, as do I, that we can learn not to be angry and out of sorts just because the world and people around us may not always be ideal. An eye for an eye is not the right response.

His studies also showed a reduction in the emotional and physical manifestations of stress and an increase in vitality when we practise forgiveness. Forgiveness decreases hurt, anger, depression and blood pressure. He believes that when we don't forgive, our mind and body are disrupted, giving the offender huge power over us.

When we forgive, we take our power back – many people don't realise this. If we don't forgive, this becomes part of our story and we continue to bring negative experiences into our future. We have templates wired into us such as revenge, anger and destruction. We need to tap into the template of forgiveness. We need to remember that forgiveness is not the same as reconciliation, or even about having to have a relationship with that person. You are just choosing to release the bitterness that you have created in yourself. This can create inner peace as you are no longer blaming others for problems in your life.

> *Forgiveness is giving up the hope that the past could have been any different, it's accepting the past for what it was, and using this moment and this time to help you move forward.*
> —Oprah Winfrey

When we make a grievance against something based on a past experience, how can we live in the present and the future? Ponder this if you feel there is something you need to let go of to serve you to move forward, in or out of the workplace.

Why is forgiveness hard?

So, if forgiveness can result in improved mental health, self-esteem, relationships and connection and less stress, anxiety and hostility, why is it so hard for us to forgive?

Many people find forgiveness difficult as they:

- don't know where to start
- come from a place of blame
- choose to complain
- live in the past and bring grievances into their future
- hold onto bitterness as it feels like justice
- believe forgiveness gives the other person power
- aren't aware of the toxicity and consequences of not forgiving
- believe forgiveness means reconciliation or justification.

Poison to peace

Along with the widely researched benefits of forgiveness, I believe it also:

- releases negative thoughts that waste headspace and energy
- enables us to focus on moving forward and what's important
- helps us to learn about ourselves at a deeper level
- teaches us gratitude
- builds resilience and adaptability
- cancels out 'awfulising' thoughts
- frees up our choices, feelings and actions.

Forgiveness requires us to have a full heart. We need to be strong, open, brave and resilient, and show vulnerability and empathy. Brené Brown talks about these qualities belonging to 'whole-hearted people'. Many people are too weakened by their hurt to be in a position to forgive. Consciously taking the right steps towards forgiveness will kick off the process of living life from a position of strength, rather than weakness.

To forgive is to let go, and to let in the energy, headspace and time to go through the process. We can't truly move forward until we do this. Failing to forgive is like putting a 4-metre fence around you that feels higher every day. We aren't all born with a forgiving nature; I believe our capacity to forgive comes from our culture, experiences, reference points and values. We are all learning organisms who can practise forgiveness. In turn, this will influence our perceptions and what we create. We have that choice.

The six keys to forgiveness

Along with the other tips, tools and ideas woven throughout this chapter, here are six keys to unwrap your past, present or future Gift of Forgiveness.

1. Identify and acknowledge your hurt

It's important to know the source of the hurt or betrayal you are living with. It may have been a person, a situation or even a missed opportunity. Take the time to tap into how this has impacted you. It could be something from your past that is affecting you today, or something you are experiencing currently. Remember the biggest gifts can be Pass the Parcel gifts: you never know what you are going to get until you unwrap them. Take the time to acknowledge how you are feeling and recognise your thoughts towards it.

2. Forgive yourself

All forgiveness starts from within. You cannot fully forgive another if you are holding them hostage in your mind. It can be easy to believe you are the reason you were hurt or betrayed, but you won't have the capacity to forgive others until you release these feelings and thoughts. Now is the time to reconnect with the present; the past has gone. Realising that everything that has happened, good or bad, has been pivotal to you becoming the person you are today lightens the load and paves the way to self-forgiveness. Shift your thoughts and feelings towards the positive and the present.

3. Change your story

Trying to forgive someone is like trying to give up a negative habit: until you change your underlying beliefs, it's almost impossible. The things we tell ourselves shape our beliefs and then create the story we live by. Take the time to revisit your beliefs around the story you hold in the context of what needs to be forgiven. If you believe a particular person is out to get you, that's all you will notice and invite in. If you believe what happened was a result of them going through a hard time, you may look at the situation from a different perspective and be more open to forgive. You are the narrator of your life – your thoughts dictate the feelings you experience and the action you do or don't take.

4. Develop a forgiving mind through empathy

Empathy and compassion will result in action when we let go of the hurt and problem, and focus on the solution of forgiveness. Practise self-compassion and also compassion for the other person. By practising empathy you are 'feeling into' the other person – whether you believe what happened was wrong or right is irrelevant. We can forgive others in many ways, depending on where we are and how we want the relationship to be moving forward. Sometimes reconciliation is not an option and you may forgive with your heart and mind but not contact the person directly. Other times you may converse with the person and show empathy. The key is, when you get to a place of forgiveness in your mind and heart, you are freeing yourself and inviting peace into your life.

5. Seek support

As Zamil said many times, we need support around us – and often the right people and resources will emerge when we are ready to forgive. I believe in seeking out those who may support you, such as friends, work colleagues and family. If you know someone who has been on a similar path, a conversation with them can be priceless. Tap into resources such as reading and inspirational podcasts, which can equip you with motivation and supportive insights. Keep in mind that there is no magic pill or remedy – we need to access what works for us, and be open to learning throughout the process. That is the gift we can unwrap for ourselves and share with others.

6. Practise gratitude

The Gift of Forgiveness is one of the most powerful ways to empower growth – not just for the forgiver, but also for the forgiven. When we let go of the poison and come to a place of peace, we have the best chance to live our best life and focus on what we have, rather than what we don't have or what isn't perfect. Problems and challenges are amplified when we are not at peace. If you are in the process of forgiveness, focus on the things you are grateful for as these can usually outweigh the resentment, anger or betrayal you may be experiencing. We always have something we can be in gratitude for. Early in my corporate career, I forgave a co-worker and thanked him for the lessons I had learnt and the strength the situation had given me. He was taken aback and ended up apologising as he knew my gratitude was genuine, and this made him open up to the situation.

> *Unforgiveness is that quality of being stuck with a mind that has found a problem, but can't solve it.* —Fred Luskin

Now it's time to unwrap your GIFT of Forgiveness

Take some time to think about the questions below.

G Grow

- What key lessons has the gift taught you?
- In what ways has it helped you to learn and grow?

I Integrate

- How will you incorporate these lessons into your life moving forward?
- What do you need to be aware of and what could get in the way of you actioning these lessons?

F Facilitate

- What lessons from this gift can you share with others professionally or personally?
- Who will you share these with and how will you share this gift?

T Transform

- How will you know that this gift has transformed you and others?
- When will you share this gift with others?

Your Forgiveness Bomboniera

- Forgiveness is a conscious and deliberate decision and can be a process and an emotion. Forgiveness doesn't always mean justifying another person's actions or a situation.
- Living a life where we hold onto anger, stress and resentment can negatively impact our physical, mental and emotional wellbeing. Studies have shown that forgiveness reduces stress and can increase vitality.
- Acceptance is the portal to forgiveness – taking the time to acknowledge and identify both the cause and our feelings allows us to choose how we want to forgive and what we need to do.
- Start by fostering a space for self-forgiveness. You are the narrator of your story, so take stock of what you are telling yourself and write a new story to move you, and potentially others, forward.
- Be light on yourself when unwrapping the Gift of Forgiveness. The way in which we practise forgiveness is as unique to us as our fingerprints. The process and time taken, and the type of support we need, will differ depending on the situation, the priority we place on it, our past experiences and our openness and intention to forgive.

Seventeen

THE GIFT OF CONTRIBUTION

> *We ourselves feel that what we are doing is just a drop in the ocean. But the ocean would be less because of that missing drop.*
> —Mother Teresa

Contribution is a core human need. Contributing to both ourselves and others can assist us in leading a more satisfying and purposeful life.

Contribution is the gift that keeps on giving, and can create a legacy that touches others and enables them to contribute themselves.

As we explore the Gift of Contribution we will unwrap::

- the four keys to the Gift of Contribution
- the areas and ways you can contribute to achieve purpose, balance and fulfilment
- the GIFT process to unwrap your Gift of Contribution and share it.

First, I'll share an excerpt from an interview I conducted for our Limitless Leaders podcast with CEO and Founder of St Kilda

Mums, Jessica Macpherson OAM. St Kilda Mums (SKM) is a not-for-profit organisation established to pass on preloved baby clothes and nursery furniture to Victorian families needing assistance. Formed in 2009, it grew from a weekly working bee held in Jessica's living room to a thriving organisation consisting of 2500 volunteers redistributing more than 60,000 nursery items annually.

Jessica's story

In early 2009 Jessica visited the St Kilda Maternal and Child Health Centre to offer a few things that her son had outgrown. She had seen families entering the clinic who looked like they might be struggling.

The nurse asked her to pop them in the photocopying room, but when Jessica opened the door, the photocopier was buried under plastic bags. The problem was the nurses didn't have time to sort or check the items that were being donated. This spurred Jessica to gather a group of girlfriends to help. They packed like with like and made up bundles of baby boy and girl clothing. They placed everything back on the shelves clearly labelled, turning a mess into a valuable resource.

Jessica and her friends felt good. They were nursing newborns themselves, constantly changing nappies and dealing with two year olds' daytime sleep patterns. But they could see how this could make a difference to the nurses' everyday work; they wanted to do more of it. So they shared their skills, and it grew from there. Today SKM's volunteers service workshops in Clayton, Geelong (Geelong Mums) and Ballarat (Eureka Mums).

Corporate programs to give back

Jessica saw potential in getting companies on board to give back, and designed a program to accommodate teams of corporate volunteers for an entire day. Jessica has noticed that more organisations are valuing what they call their corporate social responsibility programs – giving people the opportunity to volunteer is a way to connect their employees with great causes and make a difference. At SKM, a team of people can attack a large job that might overwhelm a couple of volunteers or a single staff member. There is no hierarchy when people are contributing together completing a task. Just because someone is the manager, or the most senior person, doesn't mean they are a leader.

The feedback SKM gets is that participants feel great about the work they did today going out to a family tomorrow. It's taking team building to a new level – doing something that contributes to the real world.

Jessica believes contribution comes from personal life, workplace and community, and the volunteer program at SKM hits all three.

Volunteering increases collaboration

A lot of hidden skills shine through when you are working outside the workplace and your usual role.

Jessica added that SKM can teach businesses about collaboration. In fact, sharing is part of their vision statement: 'A future where we waste less, share more and care for every baby and child.'

Such a simple vision statement makes it effortless to ask the right questions: Does this help? Is that wasteful? Does this help reduce waste? Is that a sharing thing to do?

Jessica mentors others from like-minded organisations, and believes collaboration is sharing best practice and replicating success, as well as what's gone wrong.

Jessica says giving often involves sacrificing resources such as time and money. If you're able to squeeze into your week some kind of volunteering or mentoring activity for a cause that you love, this is precious.

How do you communicate this gift?

In Jessica's sector, a lot of talented people serve on a variety of boards, which involves time, experience and skills. All charities, big and small, are mostly governed by volunteers.

In return for contribution, you get recognition. If you're giving at that level, the returns are the satisfaction of a job well done, the pleasure of contributing, the friendships you make and the people you meet. And if you get the opportunity to work closely with someone you admire and that turns into a friendship or a mentoring relationship, it's a win for everyone.

The ability to fundraise is critical for any charity to survive. Jessica went to a lot of fundraising events to learn quickly. The most memorable presentations she attended at these events always included stories of what went horribly wrong. We need to talk about the nitty-gritty of the experience and the lessons from our mistakes. That's the Gift Mindset.

What is contribution?

Jessica's story shows that contribution is about having a sense of service and a focus on helping others. Her story demonstrates contribution to the community through a purpose that serves many people on many levels.

When we contribute to others, we connect with the world by creating meaning in our lives and those of others.

The gift of contribution can be part of everyday life. No matter how small the contribution, it's the intention that matters. Just as you can't survive without contribution to your life and welfare from others, you may live an unfulfilled life if you are not contributing to others.

When you ask your future self to look back on your life and see whether it was lived well, and whether you are satisfied with what you have done, how would you respond right now? If your response doesn't match what you really want, this realisation can lead you to discover and action the Gift of Contribution.

> *Each of us is a unique strand in the intricate web of life and here to contribute.* —Deepak Chopra

Growth is another core human need. Contribution flows through to personal and spiritual growth – we feel satisfied, fulfilled and purposeful.

Contributing through feedback

Feedback is a great way to contribute, in and out of the workplace. Jessica believes this comes back to contribution, especially when it's constructive and positive.

Feeding forward, as I call it, is a proactive way to reinforce positive behaviours and successes, and provide learnings and the opportunity to make changes in real time.

As a leader, coaching is key as it encourages conversations that provide regular, ongoing feedback opportunities. The usual six- or 12-monthly performance review, or 'preview' as I call it, then becomes a proactive check-in, not a forum for catching people out.

The most effective leaders regularly coach their teams one on one or within a group forum. This can be done face to face or through a video platform such as Zoom or Teams.

Coaching can be an informal conversation on the fly or a formal locked-in session. If you aren't in a leadership position, remember feedback can take place at home, with friends – in fact, in any relationship.

I suggest leaders use a simple feedback model called Plus Delta.

The Plus Delta (++^^) model

The Plus Delta model, based on the fourth letter of the Greek alphabet, asks four questions. Two focus on celebrating what worked well, and two focus on change and what can be done differently.

This questioning feedback model encourages the receiver to reflect and respond, which creates deep self-awareness, ownership and action. You can then add your feedback and suggestions and drive an action plan.

Here are the four questions:

+ Overall what worked well; what is the positive?
+ What else?
^ What would you change or do differently?
^ What else?

You can also use this model to self-assess when reviewing a situation.

The four keys to contribution

To live the Gift of Contribution I believe we need to contribute to four key areas:

1. ourselves
2. our home team
3. our work team
4. our community.

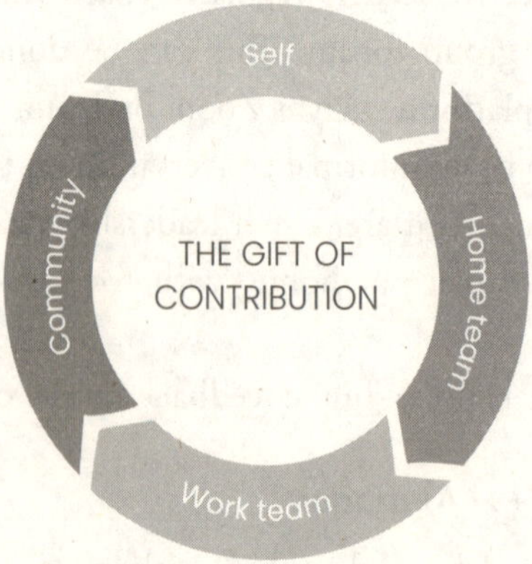

Let's look at each of these in turn.

1. Contributing to yourself

We need to serve ourselves in order to better contribute to and serve others. The saying 'you can't pour from an empty cup' applies to all of us. It's like fuelling a car – if we optimise self-contribution, the car will go further. We will feel more fulfilled and able to bring our 'whole selves' to whatever we do.

We can contribute to ourselves in a plethora of ways to ensure the Gift of Contribution doesn't remain unwrapped:

- **Look after yourself:** Mentally, spiritually and emotionally with exercise, hobbies, meditation and/or mindfulness.
- **Protect yourself:** From situations and people that disempower or drain you.
- **Grow yourself:** You will have more to contribute to others, both in and out of the workplace. Identify and develop your competencies and skills. Find out what motivates you and satisfy this – you will feel more energised.
- **Create a reading habit:** The University of Sussex found that you can reduce stress by 68% by reading for only six minutes per day. It's a great way to contribute to your growth and inner peace. Knowledge is power and reading expands your thinking.
- **Say 'thank you' with gratitude:** Accepting compliments is vital to healthy relationships. Talk to yourself like a friend and accept kind and loving thoughts.
- **Learn to say 'no' without guilt:** This can empower you and enable you to spend time on the right things and people. Trying to be everything to everyone is not sustainable. Remember you are saying 'no' to the event, not the person – this will make it easier.
- **Make time for what you love:** Think of what sparks your interest or curiosity. Maybe it's cooking or learning to play

guitar. The American Time Use Survey showed that we can find more than five hours per day for leisure time.

2. Contributing to your home team

Many of us forget the contributions we make at home, to what I call our 'home team'.

When we are giving at work, in our community and to our friends, we can leave our contributions in the lost property when it comes to our life at home. Contributing to our family and acknowledging their contributions to us is imperative for a happy, loving home environment where family life can flourish. Here's how to do it:

- **Acknowledge the good:** Catch each other out on the good things; make each other feel appreciated. Maybe your partner is being a great parent, or your child is applying themselves at school. Showing gratitude can shift your home team to the next level.
- **Be spontaneous:** Adventure and fun are the spice of life. Be the one to organise spontaneous outings, dinners, walks, bike rides or whatever floats your boat. Our lives are often planned and predictable – spontaneity can raise the energy and connection of your household.
- **Communicate openly:** Speak clearly, concisely and consistently with your partner, children or housemates. Set and share boundaries – what is okay and not okay when living together. Check in often and don't sweep unresolved issues under the rug.
- **Eat together:** Encourage discussion and sharing while contributing to making a meal for your home team, or cooking and then sharing a meal together. Food is a connector in most cultures.

- **Support each other:** The support we give and receive at home is a conduit to how connected and happy we are. Pay attention when someone needs extra support or encouragement; be open to ask for and receive support.

3. Contributing to your work team

Jessica agrees with Dale Carnegie that contributing within the workplace is not just clocking in and out – 80% of your success is actually showing up and wanting to contribute. Here's how to contribute best at work:

- **Share your passions and hobbies:** People can surprise you with hidden passions. Bring a pot plant to work and talk about your love of gardening, for example.
- **Share diverse cultures:** Bring in foods that are part of your culture; share and talk about them. Food connects – it's a great way to contribute a part of what makes you, you.
- **Create and agree on rituals:** These facilitate contribution, collaboration and a deeper understanding of each other outside work. Jessica suggests reviewing these rituals as part of the strategic planning process. Any positive business culture comes back to shared beliefs and values as a community, and rituals play a large part. Many of my clients share a word of the month or quarter and align activities, thinking and accountability to this theme.
- **Create goals:** Especially ones that push you as an individual and help your business at the same time. Progress is a key motivator for humans, so look at how you can contribute in small ways regularly. Setting clear, realistic goals with a timeline brings contribution goals to life.
- **Carve out time to contribute:** Sometimes a 10-minute conversation can change someone's thinking. Grow and

develop others by sharing your experience in an informal mentoring or coaching capacity. Give time, a valuable and powerful commodity.

- **Support others:** In the form of a conversation, feedback, advice, a shoulder to lean on or simply listening. Give back and show empathy by supporting your peers, team, customers, manager and associates in other divisions. Being supportive helps forge and maintain strong relationships and ways of working.
- **Share skills:** With individuals or teams. This can create a culture of sharing and contribution, in turn increasing motivation, morale and performance. We often have skills that we take for granted – sharing these is transferring knowledge. Think about your key skills and who may benefit from these.
- **Share ideas:** Ideas are like a living entity trapped in your mind until released, shared and brought to fruition. Leading companies are built on ideas from their employees. Toyota embraces the philosophy of *kaizen*, meaning 'change for the better'. Team members in all parts of the organisation are continuously looking for ways to improve operations, supported by people at every level in the company. Think about ways to share ideas; workshop them by setting up teams to be for and against the ideas, and then decide if they are kept or canned.

Contributing to our work team can be put aside when we get caught up in the 'doing'. People may feel like they are just a cog in the machine, so they seek fulfilment outside work, maybe volunteering or starting up their own charity or business.

Achieving your key measurables, leading a team, running meetings and so on are day-to-day duties. We can contribute by tapping into shared accountability with peers, the customer and the organisation. You'll feel more satisfaction knowing you made a difference without expecting anything in return.

4. Contributing to community

Community involvement provides a sense of belonging and social connectedness. Any effort to benefit the community is worthwhile, no matter how small. It can also offer extra meaning and purpose to your own life.

Communities can exist or be created from a shared location, hobbies, lived experiences and backgrounds, or a common cause. Even communicating with others – through online forums or social media, or in person – can help to give you a healthier mindset, improved self-worth and greater enjoyment of life.

In Australia, one-third of adults are not involved in any social or community groups. It is known that having a community to engage in and depend on, through hobbies or a social group, can help reduce the risk of mental illness.

Here are Jessica's tips for those wanting to contribute more in their community or at home:

- Volunteering Australia is a member association for organisations such as hers. They advertise volunteering opportunities.
- Update your profile on LinkedIn with your volunteering experience. Remember to include things such as surf lifesaving, children's basketball, school fetes and committees, and get recommendations if you can.
- Look at who inspires you in the workplace, or someone who you'd like to mentor, and look through their LinkedIn profile to see who that may be.
- Find charities you like and contact them to ask how to get involved.
- Contribute with family and friends to create a rich, bonding and rewarding experience.

Here's how I suggest approaching community contribution:

- **Volunteer** your time, resources, skills or money to something you believe in. This can give you purpose, fulfilment and satisfaction, and help to decrease stress and ease depression. Look at your local community and see how you can contribute. Maybe you can offer skills, networks, funding or simply time to mentor or contribute to ideas. Share your expertise to add value to others such as contributing to a non-executive board or a local sports team, charity or pet rescue centre.
- **Spread the message** of a cause you care about. Maybe it's a message you have initiated, or one created by an existing organisation that you believe in. Getting buy-in from the community is vital in paving the way for change and implementing new ideas and processes. Use your skills and networks to assist, and your influence and leadership to make an impact.
- **Organise a fundraiser** or assist with one. Offering your time, skills, network, services or products helps the fundraiser come to life. Even sharing the event and creating social awareness can help maximise its impact.
- **Mentor someone** and take them under your wing, and share your skills and experience to challenge and assist their thinking. Often, we take for granted the lessons we have learnt, when they could be a survival guide for someone else. Think about someone who could benefit and use your knowledge and experience to guide them. This could be a less experienced board member, or through a sporting or youth club. Mentorship grows both parties, whether one on one or with a group.

In the process of contributing, you will probably find you develop skills yourself – such as event planning, organisation or relationship-building skills. Putting yourself out there, whether face to face or virtually, can help grow your social skills. The more we interact with people from different walks of life, the better our adaptability and understanding of how people tick will be. This can, in turn, help us develop deeper and more meaningful interactions and relationships.

Contribute in the four areas just outlined to truly live the Gift of Contribution. Start with self-contribution and plan small ways to contribute to your home team, work team and community. Many acts of contribution flow into each other. For example, you may share the skills you build through contributing to a community project with your work team.

> *We make a living by what we get, but we make a life by what we give.* —Winston Churchill

Now it's time to unwrap your GIFT of Contribution

Take some time to think about the questions below.

G Grow

- What key lessons has the gift taught you?
- In what ways has it helped you to learn and grow?

I Integrate

- How will you incorporate these lessons into your life moving forward?
- What do you need to be aware of and what could get in the way of you actioning these lessons?

F Facilitate

- What lessons from this gift can you share with others professionally or personally?
- Who will you share these with and how will you share this gift?

T Transform

- How will you know that this gift has transformed you and others?
- When will you share this gift with others?

Your Contribution Bomboniera

- Contribution is a core human need and satisfies another human need: growth. We grow when we contribute, and we contribute through growth.
- Contribute to self through wellbeing, self-growth, reading, accepting compliments and learning to say 'no'. Dedicate time to the things that light you up.
- Look at ways to contribute to your home team through acknowledging the good, being spontaneous, and creating and sharing meals together. Keep communication open.
- Contribute to your work team by supporting others, sharing skills and giving your time. Set goals around ways to contribute and share ideas; provide feedback.
- Contribute to community by volunteering, helping spread a message, starting a fundraiser or mentoring someone who will benefit.

Eighteen

THE GIFT OF RE-ENERGISING

Rest and self-care are so important.

When you take time to replenish your spirit, it allows you to serve others from the overflow. You cannot serve from an empty vessel. —Eleanor Brownn

Living life as our full, energetic selves is vital to function at our highest level, both physically and mentally.

In this chapter, we will look at what stifles our energy at work and personally, and reflect, refocus and recharge by implementing ideas and practices to inject energy into ourselves and our lives.

As we explore the Gift of Re-energising we will unwrap:

- what depletes our energy
- the process of reflecting, refocusing and recharging
- the four pillars of wellbeing
- the seven keys to re-energise
- the GIFT process to unwrap your Gift of Re-energising and share it.

To kick off, I'd like to share a story from Angela Burr, General Manager of marketing at Lactalis, centred around realising ways to re-energise herself and her team.

Angela's story

Since childhood Angela has believed that effort counts. How you show up in terms of attitude, time and personal accountability reflects the importance you place on the task. As a leader, she quickly learnt that being task-orientated is not always the most valued trait.

With experience, she realised that in the early days she was being a 'manager'. She and her team met their deadlines with work delivered to a high standard. She remembers in those times feeling like one project ended and another just started. She was living in the future, rather than the present.

Angela realised that when she and her team focused on the 'how' rather than the 'what', they all felt a stronger sense of accomplishment.

Letting go of limiting beliefs

Angela now views her role as a leader to guide, support and encourage others. Although the task is important, it is an outcome of how she and her team are 'being', so she has shifted her focus accordingly.

To make this shift, Angela had to let go of some beliefs she was carrying about what constitutes 'doing a good job'. This involved giving herself space at work to invest time in developing relationships, listening to and encouraging others.

Angela's family is important, and she gives it the time and attention it needs. Angela is open with her work team about how she manages her time, and encourages them to be flexible with their own time to achieve work–life balance. Her experience has been that her contribution to work and her children's lives is greater when she allows herself more flexibility. At work she achieves more than she did in earlier days when task orientation was her focus, and she feels her life is also in better balance.

'Take two for you'

Angela had seen some of her team members struggle to find the same balance she had achieved. Some were not allowing themselves flexibility in managing their time, holding onto task-centric beliefs or lacking disciplined planning to put together the jigsaw of work and personal life. Angela realised talking about how they could support each other was important, so she organised a catch-up. Together they came up with 'take two for you', where everyone can take any two hours, each month, to do anything they like towards gaining work–life balance and re-energising themselves.

As a team, they take the time to share what they are doing. Those letting the opportunity to 'take two for you' slip are encouraged to take it up so everyone feels it is acceptable – in fact, expected – to do so. Angela finds it interesting that despite this she still hears team members say they haven't got time to take those two hours for themselves. This has opened up interesting conversations about why that is, and what they might need to let go of or let in to take two for themselves. As a leader, Angela has continued to encourage this practice by letting people know when she's doing her 'take two for you', and also having some tough conversations about personal accountability.

Ultimately, Angela believes leaders have a role to open doors and encourage others, no matter what their outlook or way of being. She has found the 'take two for you' idea is a springboard into coaching, as well as giving much-needed time and flexibility, and re-energising her team physically and mentally.

I love how Angela re-energised and created balance in her own life, as well as encouraging her team members to do the same for themselves. This openness and sharing of best practice was accepted by her team as something they could implement, with permission as a team to do so.

Workplace energy depletion is a reality

When someone is energised, you can feel their energy. When a work team is energised, members feel they can achieve almost anything. As a leader, if you see a gap in the energy in your team, as Angela did, you need to open the door to explore this as a team and see what is going on. Energy, or lack thereof, can be due to something deeper, so this needs to be delved into.

These days, people are working more hours and feeling stressed out, exhausted and overwhelmed at work – 'burnt out'. The World Health Organization recently deemed burnout as a classifiable workplace phenomenon.

Many factors lead to energy depletion and burnout. Some causes bridge home and the workplace, while other pressures are work-specific. The Mayo Clinic researched stress and burnout at work and has shown common workplace factors that contribute to it. I have listed a few below, in conjunction with my experiences working in organisations over the last 15 years. Here are the main contributing factors I have observed:

- **Unclear role expectations and purpose:** This can lead to lack of direction, where you question your own as well as your manager's expectations of you. An unclear purpose leads to an unclear strategy and unknown authority in your role, which can be confusing and demotivating.
- **Dysfunctional workplace dynamics:** Lack of purpose, morale or collaboration can be stressful and energy-draining. Unclear expectations of the team and organisation are confusing, along with dealing with team members who may be bullies or micromanagers.

- **Work–life imbalance:** Channelling most of your focus and energy into the workplace results in lack of energy to spend quality time on other things that matter – family, friends or passions and self-growth.
- **Job function overload:** Getting fewer people to do more not only creates an issue in the capacity to do a good job, but can also create gaps in capability. This leaves us feeling inadequate and unmotivated, especially if there is no upskilling or support.
- **Lack of control or resources:** An inability to influence decisions that affect your job – such as your schedule, assignments or workload – could lead to job burnout. So could a lack of the resources you need to do your work.
- **Extremes of activity:** When a job is monotonous or chaotic, the constant energy required to remain focused may lead to fatigue, lack of energy and job burnout.
- **Lack of social support:** A strong support network is vital. Feeling isolated at work or in your personal life might lead to feeling more stressed. Strong working relationships are key to building resilience, self-confidence and energy.

Re-energising as a leader

As a leader, you need to exude the kind of energy you want to see in others. When I led corporate teams and now, as a leader in my business, staying true to my purpose has been key to keeping my energy, and that of others, in flow.

Whether you're in a leadership role or not, you are responsible for leading yourself. Think about what energises you and start there. Be open about any concerns you have with your peers, manager or co-workers in other areas of the business. Get clear on your purpose, and your expectations of yourself and others.

Here are four questions to ask:

1. What is the expectation of my role? Be specific and get clear on this.
2. What is the expectation of my team?
3. What is the team expectation of me?
4. What is the expectation and purpose of the organisation?

If you need to re-energise, get support from those around you – whether in or outside the workplace. We all need a strong support network; remember, connection is an innate human need. Reach out to co-workers, loved ones, external mentors and friends.

Re-energising on a personal level

When we feel energised, we feel motivated on a physical, mental and emotional level. It is up to us to be aware of when and how to replenish our energy.

Life can be stressful and full of chaos – like catching spinning plates. From family, friends, work, technology and new ideas to our physical and mental health, we face conflicting priorities daily. Working long hours, lacking quality sleep and food, a manic mind and stress can zap our energy. Like a battery, we cannot be charged unless we fill our reserves.

When our energy is depleted, we are no good to anyone. Ignoring a bout of low energy can lead to adverse outcomes such as depression, illness and lack of social contact. We cannot be our whole selves if we don't take the time to re-energise.

In 1987, while completing Year 10 at school, I became tired, weak and unable to keep my eyes open in the classroom. I felt like a butterfly who had lost her wings. My throat was so sore I would wake up with blood in my mouth. I was eventually diagnosed with glandular fever. My amazing mum waited on me hand and foot for months of being bedridden. I made a full recovery and, bizarrely, since then I've had so much energy my nickname is 'Popcorn'.

I'm not sure if this experience made me want to make the most of every minute or if I am more aware of my energy levels because of it – perhaps a combination. I know when I am feeling depleted. When this happens, I tap into things that energise me such as reading, cooking, travel, catching up with family and friends, or going for a walk along the beach. Sometimes it's as simple as having a sleep-in or reflecting on my purpose to check I am on track. I am passionate about my work, which involves giving and growing others. I'm aware I need to serve myself to be effective in my work and to function wholly.

I learnt the Gift of Re-energising by hitting rock bottom in my energy reserves. Tapping into that experience keeps me accountable for staying re-energised.

Energy check-in

Whether in a professional or personal context, your energy is king. Use the process below as a simple check-in.

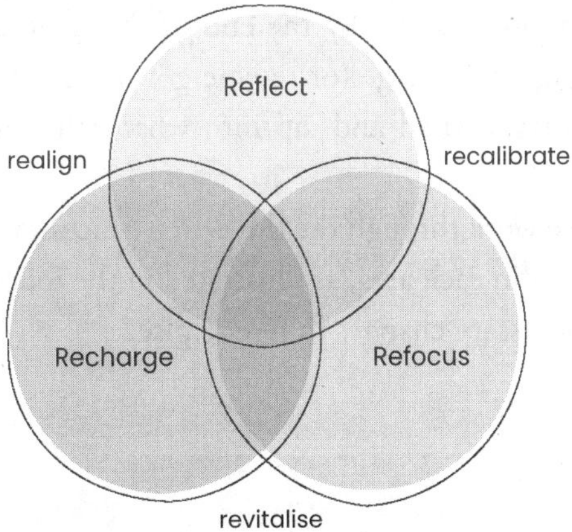

Reflect

Make it a habit to create a regular practice of self-reflection. This will create a space for self-awareness and help you to be in touch with when your energy needs replenishing. Knowing what being fully re-energised feels like for you will make it easier to identify when you are feeling depleted and need to act. Be aware of what has energised you in the past, and what and who depletes your energy.

Refocus

You can now refocus on what you need to do to re-energise. Think about what is depleting you. Maybe you're working too many hours and lacking sleep and peace of mind. Maybe you aren't living on purpose or your values are misaligned. Maybe certain people are draining your energy and you are giving too much of yourself.

Recharge

We can only re-energise when we find a compelling reason to do so. Unfortunately, for many people, this only happens when they are burnt out, stressed or ill. Take the time to feed your soul and do the things that put a pep back in your step.

Every person will be re-energised differently – do what works for you. My hope is that by the end of this chapter, your Gift of Re-energising will emerge (or re-emerge). Look back to when you felt the most energised and tap into what you were doing at the time.

When we work through the three-step process, we need to apply targeted effort in each area, as illustrated in the following model, to create the necessary changes to re-energise.

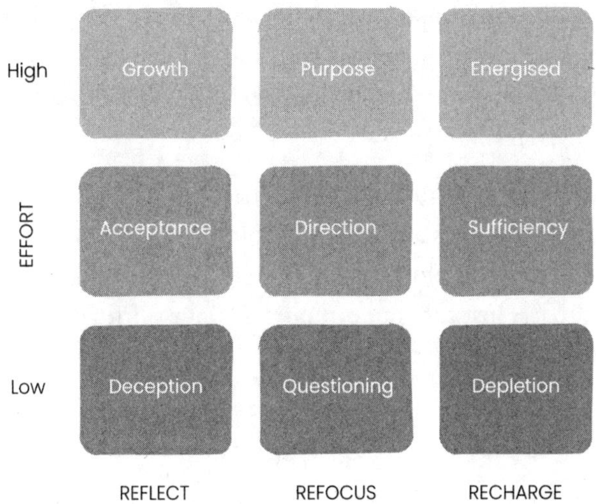

The four pillars of wellbeing

We need balance across the four key areas that feed into our energy. Wellbeing is often thought of as pertaining only to our health, but it's more than that. It really is about 'what's good for you' as a whole – when we are whole, we are re-energised. We need to 'budget' our energy in each of the four areas in order to create balance.

Looking at the four pillars can help identify what needs attention and action. Take a few minutes to reflect on the four pillars of wellbeing and what they mean to you. If you are living life with high energy, what would you be seeing, doing and feeling in each area?

1. **Emotional wellbeing:** Awareness of your emotional state involves identifying your inner dialogue and how you budget your mental energy. Emotional maturity is vital – this can help you manage stress while fostering self-compassion and kindness.

2. **Physical wellbeing:** This is about being kind to your body and aware of how it feels day to day. Create habits and routines to ensure you have a physical release.

3. **Social wellbeing:** Supportive relationships, social networking, a challenging career that grows you, and enjoying your own company support social wellbeing. Have boundaries and support systems in place.
4. **Spiritual wellbeing:** Your higher self needs to deal with things such as unforgiveness and building your belief system – 'soul work'. Having time alone, connecting to yourself and creating a sacred space, just for you, can nurture your spiritual wellbeing.

The seven keys to re-energising

The following tips will re-energise you and help you bring your whole self to whatever you do.

1. Live with purpose

Research has found that knowing your true purpose can lead to greater health and wellbeing, and exceptional performance due to role clarity. Knowing the bigger picture of why you do what you do can energise you deeply. Purpose springs from your identity – it's your 'why to fly'.

Our purpose can change, go off-track or be hidden, but it is always there. Many of my clients ask, 'How do I know if I'm living my purpose?' The answer is, only you can know this. Finding passion in what you do and knowing your 'why' is the key.

Purpose gives you direction and meaning and, therefore, it should be congruent with what you value. You need to align your greater purpose and the purpose of your team with the purpose of the organisation you work in.

2. Do what lights you up

When we tap into doing the things that motivate us, we can't help but feel lit up. Motivation is like a firework, reaching its full potential when lit up in the sky. In a work context, based on the iWAM profiling tool research, motivation can predict up to 65% of our success in a role, so it's powerful to know what motivates us. Tapping into what brings you joy, in and outside work, raises your energy – even when you feel depleted.

Here's a simple method for finding and focusing on the things that light you up:

- **Identify:** What do you love doing the most? What are you good at and enjoy doing in work and in your personal time? (These can also be the things that feel easy to you.)
- **Satisfy:** How will you incorporate the things you love into your role, and your life outside work? Remember, you can control more than you think by planning, setting boundaries and resetting these regularly.
- **Amplify:** What can you do to consistently bring the things that light you up into your life? Remember, when we are energised and doing what is congruent to us in and out of work we can't but help but be lit up and live life on purpose.

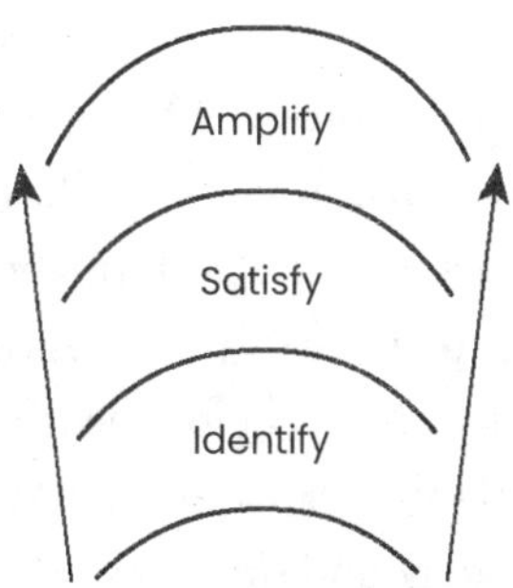

3. Think positive self-thoughts and practise gratitude

What we tell ourselves creates how we feel and then what we do or don't action. Where our thoughts go, our energy flows. If you've been thinking disempowering thoughts or focusing on what you *don't* have, your energy will reduce; you may feel drained and flat. Control your inner dialogue to serve your energy positively. Focus on what you *do* have and foster an attitude of gratitude. Talk to yourself like a friend – we are often our harshest critics. Name your inner critic when it shows up and catch out the thoughts you need to let go of.

4. Exercise and sleep well

Regular physical activity can help you better deal with stress. It can also take your mind off work. Exercise can fight fatigue and boost energy, and as little as 15 minutes a day can have significant positive health effects. A walk may be better than a nap for boosting energy and fighting fatigue, especially to break up intense work hours.

Research suggests regular exercise can increase energy levels even among people suffering from chronic medical conditions associated with fatigue, such as cancer and heart disease. Jealously plan and protect the time to do a form of exercise that works for you. I find a 20-minute walk each day increases my energy and clears my head – ultimately, I'm more productive after some movement between long stints of work.

A good night's sleep restores wellbeing and helps protect your health. Research shows that poor sleep has immediate negative effects on your hormones, exercise performance, brain function and energy. We need sleep to re-energise. Reduce blue-light (technology) exposure at least two hours before bedtime; reduce caffeinated drinks from mid-afternoon; sleep and wake at consistent times; and sleep in a room that is dark and quiet.

5. Fuel up with food

What we put into our body directly impacts our health and energy. The best energising foods are rich in complex carbohydrates, protein, antioxidants, fibre, vitamins and minerals, plus small amounts of healthy fats. This balanced diet is sure to provide energy all day long. Work travel, early starts, late nights, long hours and too much coffee can stifle our good intentions. Eating nourishing foods is a great habit to adopt, reviewing and renewing if we go off-track.

6. Get outside and get grounded

Many studies have shown that even looking at a photograph of the natural environment can cause your stress levels to drop and your mood and energy levels to improve. The reason for this is that your brain dials itself down and rests – it understands that a natural environment, whether real or in a picture, contains complex sensory inputs and so it refuses to make sense of it, and therefore relaxes. Getting out in nature for a beach walk, bike ride, swim or gardening – or even eating lunch outside – can do wonders for your energy reserves.

Grounding, also known as earthing, has been proven to help reduce stress and even pain, according to the *Journal of Environmental and Public Health*. The theory is that because we spend so much time indoors, we have become disconnected from nature. All it takes to reconnect is to make direct contact with the earth. Think about walking on a fresh lawn or a sandy beach in bare feet – this exposes us to the earth's electrons, which make us feel more balanced and energised.

7. Practise mindfulness

The best way I have found to describe mindfulness is that it's the quality of being present and fully engaged in whatever we are doing. In this state, we are free from judgement and distraction, and aware of our thoughts and feelings. For some, mindfulness may occur through breath and meditation; for others, like me, it may be through writing or cooking a meal for loved ones. Mindfulness re-energises us; I liken it to that feeling after daydreaming. In a job setting, mindfulness may involve facing situations with openness and patience, and without judgement. Any mindful practice needs to consist of three parts: your intention and what you hope to get from it; the attention you are paying to your experience; and the attention you give to certain attitudes, such as curiosity and acceptance.

To adopt a Gift Mindset and tap into the Gift of Re-energising, we need to deepen our awareness of our energy and know what feeling energetic is like, compared to feeling depleted. We need to then accept what is going on in order to re-energise. Lastly, we need to look at what we can do to re-energise ourselves.

Now it's time to unwrap your GIFT of Re-energising

Take some time to think about the questions below.

G Grow

- What key lessons has the gift taught you?
- In what ways has it helped you to learn and grow?

I Integrate

- How will you incorporate these lessons into your life moving forward?
- What do you need to be aware of and what could get in the way of you actioning these lessons?

F Facilitate

- What lessons from this gift can you share with others professionally or personally?
- Who will you share these with and how will you share this gift?

T Transform

- How will you know that this gift has transformed you and others?
- When will you share this gift with others?

Your Re-energising Bomboniera

- Re-energising is vital to be our best selves. Having deep awareness of when and how to re-energise is key. It's important to reflect, refocus and recharge to restore our energy.
- In the workplace, know what 'good' energy looks like for you and your team. If you notice a gap in energy in your team or peers, you need to open the door to explore this and see what is going on.
- When we re-energise, we need to tap into the four pillars of our wellbeing – physical, emotional, social and spiritual – to ensure balance.
- Get clear on your purpose and identify and amplify the things that motivate you. Practise positive self-talk to reinforce progress and positivity, and practise gratitude.
- Plan and protect time to focus on your physical health with nutritious food, quality sleep and exercise. Get out in nature. Practise mindfulness to stop, be present and replenish your cup.

EPILOGUE

Well, here we are, coming to the final pages! Congratulations for making your way through and for opening up your mind and heart to the Gift Mindset. I finish writing this book with a glimmer of sadness, but at the same time I feel immense excitement and heartfelt gratitude to be able to share this and see people, like you, and organisations embrace and action what is often swept under the carpet.

What's next? Just make a start!

As you read the final pages of this book, it is really just the start of applying what you have learnt and discovered to now open, unwrap and share your gifts with the world. Now you need to bring in the practice of the Gift Mindset and make reflective time to deepen your awareness, acceptance and understanding of the lessons you have gleaned, through both negative and positive experiences. I know that when we do this, we can apply these lessons for ourselves and those around us. Challenge yourself by asking, 'What will it cost me or my team *not* to do this?'

The concepts, ideas and experiences I have shared in this book have been in my thinking for a few years. To be able to express and share my ideas has felt like a gift in itself. I am so grateful to those people who have shared and woven their stories and insights into the tapestry that makes up the 12 Gifts.

My intention for writing this book was to provide a resource that you can tap into and access at any time with models, processes, stories and examples. Bring in the GIFT model of questioning as an easy-to-follow, structured way to unwrap and share anything that has resonated with you.

Share this book and your learnings with your team and loved ones and use it as a guide to work through and in return help others unwrap their gifts.

Remember, sharing your gifts and the lessons you have learnt could be a survival guide for others and can help you transform an event you have encountered into an experience that, once unwrapped, can be shared and a part of your living legacy.

By cultivating a Gift Mindset, in the pathway below that we worked through earlier, we can transition from being unaware to limitless. We can move from a place of inertia and being caught up in the daily drift of life to better engagement with ourselves and others, leading to more success.

Cultivating a Gift Mindset

INDIVIDUAL OR ORGANISATION POSITION	BEHAVIOUR	FOCUS	SUCCESS FACTOR
Legacy	Limitless	Engagement	x 10
Revealed	Fearless	Education	x 5
GIFT MINDSET® CULTURE			
Unwrapped	Courageous	Experience	x 2
Untied	Limited	Event	x 1.5
Wrapped	Unaware	Inertia	x 1

The Gift Mindset is a key trait of any Limitless Leader™, whether you are leading a team or not. I have enjoyed teaching the concepts in this book in many of our transformational leadership and communication programs and I look forward to continuing to share what is possible when we embrace and express the lessons we glean in our lives.

Working with thousands of leaders and teams across 24 industries, I've observed that the highest-performing organisations embrace a purpose-driven, human-centric culture. These organisations are open to providing a safe space that allows people to share and learn from mistakes and successes – in other words, they adopt the Gift Mindset.

Life gets busy; we all are faced with conflicting priorities to juggle, but we need to be the change. We need to go from suppressing our gifts to expressing them by carefully removing the wrapping. We can then expose the magic that is within us.

Thanks for investing in the time to read this book and I hope that the value you have received is now ready to be taken from 'knowing' to 'action' – acting on what you have learnt and bringing this into your leadership and life is imperative to make the Gift Mindset and all its magic three-dimensional.

I love the quote by Aristotle: 'For the things we have to learn before we can do them, we learn by doing them.'

My gift to you is now unwrapped and in your hands.

Renée
reneegiarrusso.com

REFERENCES AND FURTHER READING

Chapter 1

N Cameron (2020), 'Brene Brown: What it takes to be a brave leader right now', CMO, cmo.com.au/article/682135/brene-brown-what-it-takes-brave-leader-right-now.

L Festinger (1954), 'A theory of social comparison processes', *Human Relations*, vol. 7, pp. 117–140.

C Hymas (2018), 'A decade of smartphones: we now spend an entire day every week online', *The Telegraph*, telegraph.co.uk/news/2018/08/01/decade-smartphones-now-spend-entire-day-every-week-online.

Lifeline (2020), 'Data and statistics', lifeline.org.au/resources/data-and-statistics.

S Lyubomirsky (2008), *The How of Happiness: A New Approach to Getting the Life You Want*, Penguin Group.

S Turkle (2017), *Alone Together*, Basic Books, 2017.

Chapter 3

J Clear (2018), *Atomic Habits*, Century.

Chapter 4

K Benson (2017), 'The Magic Relationship Ratio, According to Science', The Gottman Institute, gottman.com/blog/the-magic-relationship-ratio-according-science.

H Bresman (2012), 'Changing Routines: A Process Model of Vicarious Group Learning in Pharmaceutical R&D', *Academy of Management Journal*, vol. 56, no. 1.

B Fredrickson & M Losada (2005), 'Positive affect and the complex dynamics of human flourishing', *The American Psychologist*, vol. 60, no. 7, pp. 678–86.

D Goleman (1996), *Emotional Intelligence: Why It Can Matter More Than IQ*, Bloomsbury.

MA Killingsworth & DT Gilbert (2010), 'A Wandering Mind Is an Unhappy Mind', *Science*, 330 (6006).

PD MacLean (1990), *The Triune Brain in Evolution: Role in Paleocerebral Functions*, Springer.

A Mehrabian (1971), *Silent messages*, Wadsworth Publishing Company.

C Myers (2017), 'Is Your Company Encouraging Employees to Share What They Know?', *Harvard Business Review*, hbr.org/2015/11/is-your-company-encouraging-employees-to-share-what-they-know.

Udemy (2018), *Udemy In Depth: 2018 Workplace Distraction Report*, research.udemy.com/research_report/udemy-depth-2018-workplace-distraction-report.

Chapter 5

CareerBuilder (2011), 'Seventy-One Percent of Employers Say They Value Emotional Intelligence Over IQ, According to CareerBuilder Survey', press.careerbuilder.com/2011-08-18-Seventy-One-Percent-of-Employers-Say-They-Value-Emotional-Intelligence-Over-IQ-According-to-CareerBuilder-Survey.

L Cazaly (2019), *ish: The Problem with our Pursuit for Perfection and the Life-Changing Practice of Good Enough*, Cazaly Communications (Cazcom).

P Chödrön (2019), *Welcoming the Unwelcome*, Shambhala.

D Goleman (1996), *Emotional Intelligence: Why It Can Matter More Than IQ*, Bloomsbury.

C Heath (2007), *Made to Stick: Why Some Ideas Survive and Others Die*, Random House.

K Neff (2011), *Self-Compassion*, William Morrow.

P Salovey & JD Mayer (1990), 'Emotional Intelligence', *Imagination, Cognition and Personality*, vol. 9, no. 3, pp. 185–211.

D Siegel (2009), *Mindsight: Change Your Brain and Your Life*, Scribe Publications.

Chapter 7

Beyond Blue (2020), 'The facts', beyondblue.org.au/the-facts.

R Iger (2019), *The Ride of a Lifetime: Lessons Learned from 15 Years as CEO of the Walt Disney Company*, Random House.

E Kim (2020), Eric S. Kim, ericskim.com.

J Oh, WJ Chopik & ES Kim (2020), 'The association between actor/partner optimism and cognitive functioning among older couples', *Journal of Personality*, vol. 88, no. 4, pp. 822–832.

Rozanski et al. (2019), 'Association of Optimism With Cardiovascular Events and All-Cause Mortality: A Systematic Review and Meta-analysis', *JAMA Network Open*, vol. 2, no. 9.

MF Scheier & CS Carver (1992), 'Effects of optimism on psychological and physical well-being: Theoretical overview and empirical update', *Cognitive Therapy and Research*, vol. 16, no. 2, pp. 201–228.

MF Scheier, CS Carver & MW Bridges (2001), 'Optimism, pessimism, and psychological well-being', in EC Chang (Ed.), *Optimism & pessimism: Implications for theory, research, and practice*, American Psychological Association.

MEP Seligman (1991), *Learned Optimism*, AA Knopf.

PG van der Velden et al. (2007), 'The association between dispositional optimism and mental health problems among disaster victims and a comparison group: a prospective study', *Journal of affective disorders*, vol. 102, no. 1–3, pp. 35–45.

J Weitzer et al. (2020), 'The contribution of dispositional optimism to understanding insomnia symptomatology: Findings from a cross-sectional population study in Austria', *Journal of Sleep Research* (forthcoming).

L Wood (2020), 'A Media Diet that Limits Negative News', IdeaSpies, ideaspies.com/post/2972.

Chapter 8

Brené Brown (2019), *The Call to Courage*, Netflix.

A Horowitz (2011), '15 People Who Were Fired Before They Became Filthy Rich', *Business Insider Australia*, businessinsider.com.au/15-people-who-were-fired-before-they-became-filthy-rich-2011-4.

Chapter 9

EA Greenfield (2009), 'Felt obligation to help others as a protective factor against losses in psychological well-being following functional decline in middle and later life', *The journals of gerontology, Series B, Psychological sciences and social sciences*, vol. 64, no. 6, pp. 723–732.

Harvard University, 'Resilience', developingchild.harvard.edu/science/key-concepts/resilience.

E Kacewicz, R Slatcher & J Pennebaker (2006), 'Expressive Writing: An Alternative to Traditional Methods', in L L'Abate (Ed.), *Low-Cost Approaches to Promote Physical and Mental Health*, Springer.

SR Maddi (2004), 'Hardiness: An Operationalization of Existential Courage', *Journal of Humanistic Psychology*, vol. 44, no. 3, pp. 279–298.

N Zhang (2014), 'Can Purpose Keep You Alive?', *Greater Good Magazine*, greatergood.berkeley.edu/article/item/can_purpose_keep_you_alive.

Chapter 10

SB Algoe, SL Gable & NC Maisel (2010), 'It's the little things: Everyday gratitude as a booster shot for romantic relationships', *Personal Relationships*, vol. 17, pp. 217–233.

H Craig (2020), '41+ Gratitude Messages, Letters and Lists', PositivePsychology, positivepsychology.com/gratitude-messages-letters-lists.

R Emmons (2008), *Thanks! How Practicing Gratitude Can Make You Happier*, Mariner Books.

ME McCullough, J Tsang & RA Emmons (2004), 'Gratitude in Intermediate Affective Terrain: Links of Grateful Moods to Individual Differences and Daily Emotional Experience', *Journal of Personality and Social Psychology*, vol. 86, no. 2, pp. 295–309.

L Waters (2012), 'Predicting Job Satisfaction: Contributions of Individual Gratitude and Institutionalized Gratitude', *Psychology*, vol. 3, no. 12A, pp. 1174–1176.

Chapter 11

DE Berlyne (1960), *Conflict, arousal, and curiosity*, McGraw-Hill Book Company.

Chapter 12

JH Fabre (1912), *The Life of the Caterpillar*.

C Heath & D Heath (2010), *Switch: How to Change Things When Change Is Hard*, Currency.

International Coach Federation, 'Research Portal', researchportal.coachfederation.org.

B Schwartz (2005), *The Paradox of Choice: Why More Is Less*, Harper Perennial.

Chapter 14

D Carnegie (1998), *How to Win Friends and Influence People*, Gallery Books.

R Dunbar (2010), *How Many Friends Does One Person Need?: Dunbar's Number and Other Evolutionary Quirks*, Faber.

S Godin (2019), 'Deep connection', Seth's Blog, seths.blog/2019/12/deep-connection.

D Goleman (1995), *Emotional Intelligence*, Bantam Books.

W Isaacson (2012), 'The Real Leadership Lessons of Steve Jobs', *Harvard Business Review*, hbr.org/2012/04/the-real-leadership-lessons-of-steve-jobs.

F Rain (2019), 'Loneliness Is Now More Deadly Than Cancer And Heart Disease', Medium, medium.com/@frankierain/loneliness-is-now-more-deadly-than-cancer-and-heart-disease-478ba6b6a652.

M Solomon (2017), 'Tony Hsieh Reveals The Secret To Zappos' Customer Service Success In One Word', *Forbes*, forbes.com/sites/micahsolomon/2017/06/12/tony-hsieh-spills-the-beans-the-one-word-secret-of-zappos-customer-service-success/#3b7665cb1acc.

A Staik (2016), 'Mirror Neurons: How Our Ability to Connect With Others Makes Us Caring, Moral By Nature', PsychCentral, blogs.psychcentral.com/relationships/2014/06/mirror-neurons-how-our-ability-to-connect-with-others-makes-us-caring-moral-by-nature.

Victorian Department of Health & Human Services (2017), 'Strong relationships, strong health', betterhealth.vic.gov.au/health/healthyliving/strong-relationships-strong-health.

Chapter 15

Businessolver (2018), '2018 State of Workplace Empathy', info.businessolver.com/empathy-2018-executive-summary.

D Goleman (2007), 'Three Kinds of Empathy: Cognitive, Emotional, Compassionate', danielgoleman.info/three-kinds-of-empathy-cognitive-emotional-compassionate.

C Palmeri & J Green (2017), 'PR Nightmares: United Fiasco Among Worst Corporate Gaffes', Bloomberg, bloomberg.com/news/articles/2017-04-12/pr-nightmares-united-seat-fiasco-among-worst-corporate-gaffes.

Chapter 16

Johns Hopkins Medicine, 'Forgiveness: Your Health Depends on It', hopkinsmedicine.org/health/wellness-and-prevention/forgiveness-your-health-depends-on-it.

Stanford University, 'Fred Luskin', vpge.stanford.edu/people/fred-luskin.

Chapter 17

Australian Government Department of Health, 'Connecting with community', headtohealth.gov.au/meaningful-life/connectedness/community.

D. Lewis (2009), Galaxy Stress Research, Mindlab International, Sussex University, UK.

US Bureau of Labor Statistics (2019), 'Average hours per day spent in selected activities by sex and day', bls.gov/charts/american-time-use/activity-by-sex.htm#.

Chapter 18

G Chevalier (2012), 'Earthing: health implications of reconnecting the human body to the Earth's surface electrons', *Journal of environmental and public health*.

Mayo Clinic (2018), 'Job burnout: How to spot it and take action', mayoclinic.org/healthy-lifestyle/adult-health/in-depth/burnout/art-20046642.

Sleep Health Foundation, sleephealthfoundation.org.au.

University of Georgia (2006), 'Regular Exercise Plays A Consistent And Significant Role In Reducing Fatigue', ScienceDaily, sciencedaily.com/releases/2006/11/061101151005.htm.

MM van den Berg et al. (2015), 'Autonomic Nervous System Responses to Viewing Green and Built Settings: Differentiating Between Sympathetic and Parasympathetic Activity', *International journal of environmental research and public health*, vol. 12, no. 12, pp. 15860–15874.

World Health Organization (2019), 'Burn-out an "occupational phenomenon": International Classification of Diseases', who.int/mental_health/evidence/burn-out/en/.

WITH GRATITUDE

The writing of this book would not have been possible without the people and experiences I have encountered in my life, these themselves being gifts. Who I am becoming and the words penned in this book are a result of my journey to date and it has been an incredible privilege to write this book.

The Gift of Gratitude is a daily practice for me, and I couldn't be more grateful than to have the opportunity to share the message of this book. It couldn't have happened without the support of such a wonderful army of people around me.

A huge thank you for the amazing team that has supported me in bringing this book to life. Thank you to my brilliant editor, Jackey Coyle, for keeping me on track, providing feedback, challenging me and really understanding my message and passion to write this book. To Lesley Williams and her incredible team at Major Street: thank you for bringing the book to completion. From the design of the cover to the final editing, to turning my less-than-artistic diagrams into illustrations – and for believing in me and this book. Thank you Tess McCabe, Brooke Lyons and Kerry Milin.

To my team within RG Dynamics who have been supporting me and our fabulous clients: thank you for keeping me on top of everything when I was working late nights and weekends on this book. Thank you Jacqui James, Annemarie Cross, Victoria Brown and Sarah Keen: you all contribute in different ways and this doesn't go unnoticed. Thanks also to Nia McMartin, who was a part of the RG Dynamics team when I birthed the idea for this book.

A big shout out to those who have been part of my business journey, including colleagues, clients and fellow thought leaders who keep me challenged and have been a sounding board I'm so appreciative of. You have all taught me the value of the ongoing Gift of Growth. Jane Anderson, you have been such a shining light as my extraordinary mentor and for this I thank you. To Peter Cook and Matt Church at Thought Leaders Business School, I have you to thank for igniting the motivation and passion within me to start my authoring journey in 2016. Thank you for your guidance and brilliant insights over the years. To my virtual mentors, colleagues and fellow business owners (you know who you are): thank you for being part of my life. Rohan Dredge, Shelley Flett and Jacquie Scammell: thank you for being in my circle.

I have so much gratitude to the amazing people who have shared their stories and insights woven into this book. Marie Varrasso, Victor Perton, Jessica Macpherson and Claire Summers, thank you for such heartfelt and rich contributions to these pages and for sharing the Gifts of Growth, Optimism, Contribution and Gratitude. Angela Burr, Zamil Chowdhury and Claudio Conte, thank you for sharing your stories on the Gifts of Re-energising, Forgiveness and Empathy. I know your stories will resonate with so many. Kate Stewart and Steven Pereira: thank you for sharing your magic on the Gifts of Curiosity and Resilience. Huge gratitude to my Aunty Flora and her daughter Skye Culpan for connecting me to the Gift of Courage through the story of our family.

Thank you to my circle of clients: the amazing Limitless Leaders and organisations we get to work with. The contributions I make through the work and the self-growth I have experienced wouldn't be possible without you.

And finally, a huge shout out to my home tribe, who are nothing short of amazing. Brett, you have always been an ongoing support and without your love, understanding and late-night coffees

I would have been lost while writing this book. Your calm and patient nature balances me, and for this I thank you. To my mum, Denise, and stepdad, Kym, your support has always allowed me to dream big and you are my two biggest gifts that keep on giving. To my sister, Lyndelle, you personify the Gift of Resilience and not a day goes by that I am not in awe of your strength and ability to move through adversity. To Dean, my brother, you encapsulate the Gift of Courage and have been a father figure to me. I thank you. To Laura, Olivia, Anthony, Marcel and Casey, my beautiful nieces and nephews, you light up my life and keep the Gift of Curiosity alive through your childlike wonder.

To my beautiful friends who have given me the gift of friendship, I love that I get to walk this life with you. Friends can come and go, and I am so blessed to have friends from early childhood – such as my bestie, Amanda Holloway – still in my life, along with those I've met in later years. You're all part of who I am.

And to you, the reader: a big thank you for investing in the time to read this book. My wish for you is that you read this with a curious mind, because this will open up new thinking and ways of looking at the way you embrace and share challenges and successes. May the art of unwrapping your 12 Gifts to live and lead your legacy be one you take with you on your journey through this thing called life.

CONTINUE YOUR GIFT OF GROWTH

Renée Giarrusso is a sought-after leadership and communication expert. She speaks, coaches, mentors and educates leaders and teams and runs transformational, tailored workshop programs. Working with thousands of leaders and executives in over 24 industries, she creates programs to match clients' needs by understanding their challenges. Her clients love her passion, wisdom, relatability, energy and commitment as well as her interactive working style.

Industries Renée has worked with include fast-moving consumer goods, building and construction, engineering, retail, consumer durables, electronics, beverage, automotive, real estate, professional services and not-for-profits.

Speaking

If you are looking for a highly dynamic speaker to inspire, inform and raise the energy of your next event, team offsite or conference, look no further. Specialising in communication, leadership, motivation and the Gift Mindset, Renée will tailor the session to your objectives, audience and timeframe. Bringing in an external speaker can really lift engagement and add variety and another perspective to your event.

Learning

Renée and her team offer a diverse range of solutions to bring learnings to life and ensure lessons are embedded and applied.

The Gift Mindset® Culture

To bring this book to life we need to adopt the Gift Mindset within the workplace to take leadership, connection and collaboration to the next level. This program, run in a learn and do environment, will run as series of interactive sessions on the concept and application of the Gift Mindset and each of the 12 Gifts.

Limitless Leaders Acceleration program

Born out of 18 years' experience at the coalface of leadership, this program is a 12-month transformational program where we collaborate as an open group of leaders working on relevant problems and opportunities in real time via a variety of workshops, groups coaching, mentoring and mastermind sessions.

Mapping Team Motivational Intelligence

This program motivates and creates a deeper understanding of each other's strengths and the utilisation of those strengths as a team. The iWAM profiling tool is the backbone of this program and learnings can be instilled straightaway to ensure motivation is leveraged.

Coaching for Performance

This interactive workshop program is targeted at leaders who are looking to further develop in the skill of coaching with a plan to implement coaching as part of their workplace culture.

Presenting with Impact

If you or your team want to upskill your presentations, whether through gaining more confidence, applying structure, delivering with impact or understanding your audience to engage and influence more effectively, this program is for you.

Skill Pills

Skill Pills are a dynamic and tailored approach to learning consisting of individual two- to three-hour sessions that can be run virtually or face to face to a wide audience.

Supercharge Working Remotely

A self-paced online program to take your remote work to the next level.

Executive coaching and mentoring

Renée and her team coach and mentor clients both one on one and within group coaching forums. Program duration and objectives are tailored to individual and organisational needs.

All coaches are credentialed by the International Coach Foundation (ICF). Renée has held an ICF Professional Certified Coach credential since 2009, and has well over 3000 coaching hours under her belt.

Stay connected

To stay inspired and in flow is a discipline. Here are a few ways to live the Gift Mindset and continue to grow your Limitless Leadership™ with Renée Giarrusso.

Resources

Download our diagnostic, white papers and other resources ready to read and consume.
reneegiarrusso.com
giftmindset.com

Read

The Limitless Leadership™ Connection Blog is your fortnightly insight to lift professional and personal performance delivered directly to your inbox. It covers a wide array of topics, including leadership, communication, culture, mindset, habits, motivation, branding and emotional intelligence.
reneegiarrusso.com/blog

Listen

Podcast

On the move? The Limitless Leaders Podcast will keep you up to date wherever you are. Renée interviews leaders, business owners and people from all walks of life. Find out how you can lead from the inside out to develop limitless self-leadership, leaders, teams and organisations. Available on Apple Podcasts, Android and Spotify.
reneegiarrusso.com/podcast-subscribe

Playlist

Some people love the quiet when working. Not me! Having noise around me keeps me motivated and in flow. Writing this book over weekends in lockdown during the pandemic I had to get creative! I've made a playlist of my favourite writing inspo tunes; you can find it on Spotify.
open.spotify.com/user/renee-362/playlist/
2Ct7IDlPqrvmmdzSw11E4H

Watch

Nudge your thinking through short videos on topics to take your leadership and life to the next level.
giftmindset.com

RECIPES TO RE-ENERGISE

Food really is like a time machine to our memories and cooking has been my passion since I was 10 years old. It allows me to make the space to create and be in flow. I've never followed recipes and cook from taste and observation. Those who know me know I am not a still person, so cooking is almost like a form of meditation to me.

Two of my favourite dishes I prepared many times while writing this book are my nonna's stuffed artichokes and one of my favourite Sri Lankan curries. I usually put pen to paper on the weekends, and nothing energised me more than taking a break to shop for and cook these dishes.

For me, the Gifts of Connection, Re-energising and Growth come through when I cook. It's not just about the act of cooking, but the connection of creating and sharing dishes made with love.

Italian stuffed artichokes

This is a recipe my nonna Sylvia used to make for us as kids. Later in life, Mum also made it for us.

I still remember my nonna's beautiful small hands lovingly stuffing each artichoke leaf. Such a labour of love. We couldn't wait to devour the tender leaves and get to the best bit: the heart of the artichoke. Being only a winter vegetable, it was a real treat. I now make these many times during the winter; not only are they delicious, but they bring back my heritage and fond childhood memories of family and love.

Ingredients

4 whole artichokes
1½ cups of fresh breadcrumbs
1 bunch of parsley, finely chopped
2 tbsp of grated parmesan cheese
8 cloves of garlic, finely chopped
2 tbsp olive oil, plus extra to serve
salt and pepper

Method

1. Wash the artichokes and peel off any dry outer leaves.
2. Cut stems off the artichokes, so they have a flat base.
3. Combine the breadcrumbs, parsley, cheese, garlic and olive oil. Mix to a moist crumb.
4. Add salt and pepper to taste.
5. Stuff artichokes separately. Pinch a small amount of stuffing and push to the base of each leaf, starting with the outer leaves.
6. Move the artichokes in a circular motion until all leaves are filled with stuffing right up until the centre where the leaves become tight.
7. Fill a large saucepan with 4cm of water. Place the artichokes in, standing up.
8. Bring to the boil and then simmer on low for one hour with lid on.
9. Artichokes are ready when outer leaves start to fall and the flesh on leaves is tender.
10. Drizzle with olive oil to serve.

Buon appetito!

Sri Lankan fish curry

This is my recipe, passed down from the elders. In my mid-teens I first tasted the magic of Sri Lankan cuisine cooked by close Sri Lankan friends and their families. I love the richness and diversity of Sri Lankan food and to this day this fish curry is in my top three meals to cook, share and eat. The pungent aroma of this cooking evokes memories of parties, friends' kitchens and carefree times exploring the colorful Sri Lankan culture.

Ingredients

Spice mix

3 tbsp coriander seeds
1 tbsp cumin seed
1½ tsp fennel seeds
1 tbsp turmeric powder
¼ tsp fenugreek seeds
3 cloves
6 black peppercorns
1 tsp chilli flakes

Other ingredients

2 tbsp coconut oil or ghee
1 large brown onion, finely chopped
2 tomatoes, finely chopped
1 clove of garlic, finely chopped
10 curry leaves
5 green cardamom pods, cracked
2.5-cm cinnamon stick
1½ tbsp yellow mustard seeds
1 tbsp tamarind puree
1½ 400ml cans of coconut cream

1 kg of white, boneless/skinless fish (trevally or barramundi works well), cut into 4cm pieces
1 lime, juiced
Salt and pepper
½ cup chopped coriander

Method

1. To make spice mix, toast spices in dry pan until aromatic. Allow to cool. Grind to a powder and set aside.
2. Heat oil in large shallow pan over medium heat.
3. Add onions, tomatoes, garlic and curry leaves. Cook until soft.
4. Add spice mix, stirring 2–3 minutes until aromatic.
5. Stir through cardamon, cinnamon and mustard seeds, followed by tamarind puree.
6. Stir in coconut cream and simmer over low heat for 15 minutes. Add water if becoming too thick.
7. Add fish pieces and simmer for 10 minutes.
8. Remove cardamon pods and cinnamon stick.
9. Add lime juice and salt and pepper to taste.
10. Garnish with coriander to serve.

Great with coconut rice, dahl or a vegetarian curry.

INDEX

WHAT OUR CLIENTS ARE SAYING

Renée is one of Australia's leading thinkers in the domain of leadership and has a profound impact on her clients. She is also generous, smart and highly committed. If you want to be in the top 15% of leaders in your field, work with Renée.

Peter Cook, Speaker, author, mentor and Chairperson of Thought Leaders

It's rare that you come across standout talent like Renée. I had the pleasure of attending both a Coaching for Excellence course and a 4ward thinking seminar that Renée facilitated. I was in awe of Renée's ability to command a room and get people on board with ideas on easy to use coaching and leadership models. Her energy and passion was so inspiring and engaging. As a trainer, coach, mentor, leader and facilitator, Renée earns my highest recommendation

Rachel Love, Relationship Director, Jones Lang Lasalle

Renée has been working with Intrax for many years now, providing great leadership insight and training to our leadership teams. Her operational experience, combined with her up to date knowledge of the area, make her someone who the team enjoy learning from and employing her teachings in their day-to-day jobs.

Barry Borzillo, Managing Director and CEO, Intrax Consulting Engineers Pty Ltd

Renée is a highly energetic and engaging speaker, facilitator and coach who demonstrates passion for her subject matter. She will work in your business to embed tools and practices to build capability and strengthen organisational performance. Renée's style is polished but down to earth, and she is adaptable and highly organised. I would thoroughly recommend Renée to work with and add value to your business.

Karen Littlepage, CPHR, Chief People & Culture Officer, GS1 Australia

I appreciate the learnings and support, for both myself and our team, received from Renée during our workshops and coaching sessions. We engaged Renée to help develop not only our senior leaders with her Limitless Leaders Acceleration program but also our future leaders, exposing them to a limitless mindset and motivational intelligence team program which has proved invaluable in our quest for constant improvement. Renée builds rapport quickly which enables her to engage with any audience easily. Wishing you every success with your book Renée!

Simon Taylor, Regional West Manager, Metricon Homes

Renée's Virtual Building Blocks workshops supported and inspired our members during challenging times this year. Her six-workshop series provided ready-to-use strategies on topics such as energising working from home, building emotional intelligence and building your own personal brand. Renée's genuinely friendly and dynamic approach encouraged everyone to take part and feel safe to share their stories. After attending the first workshop, we saw many members booking in for the whole series. We've found a warm and engaging presenter who is a pleasure to work with, and we look forward to an ongoing collaboration.

Ingrid Mountford, Careers and Registration Manager, Master Builders Association of Victoria

Renée supported me through a huge transition in my career, going from an FMCG brand owner to building my own food manufacturing site. Renée taught me many techniques on how to lead people with different skill sets, most more than my own.

Needless to say, with Renée's guidance and consistent coaching the business has not only flourished but also attracted many strong team members. Renée certainly allowed me to push through my insecurities and build a strong leadership team and therefore business.

Narelle Plapp, CEO and Founder, Grain and Bake Co

I have been working with Renée for a number of years now and the value added to my business is immense. Renée has a unique energy and genuine talent rarely seen in even effective presenters and facilitators. With her leadership experience you will get your teams and yourself to make the step from good performance to amazing performance. Renée's understanding of leadership demonstrated from her personal experience both working in and working on a broad spectrum of businesses has made her one of the best trainers, coaches and speakers you can get. I would recommend you discover just how effective Renée is.

Darryl O'Neill, General Manager – Sales, Kagome Australia

Renée has a special kind of energy and is instantly able to engage with a room full of people and keep them with her for a whole day. She is interesting, relevant, funny, caring, relatable and most of thought-provoking. My first day with Renée changed my view on leadership and took me in a different direction as a leader of a People and Culture group. I decided she was the one who I wanted to be my coach, to take me on the journey of professional and personal growth and I can say with confidence that I attribute my continued growth and success to Renée. Thank you, Renée, for always challenging me to be better, think differently and be a great leader. Your energy brings a special energy to me that others benefit from too, and I am lucky to have you as my coach.

Angie Francis, People & Culture – Group Manager,
William Adams Pty Ltd

Renée's enthusiasm for coaching, leading and mentoring is all about taking you and your team on a journey of discovering self and leading your team to higher results. The delivery from Renée is always on point and comes from a place of wanting people to succeed at work and life in general. I can't recommend Renée highly enough if you want to improve self and to take your business and teams to the next level.

Tony Gall, Regional Sales Manager – North, Metricon Homes

I have worked with Renée for seven years through RG Dynamics programs and mentoring. The energy and genuine interest that she brings to every session raises the room to a new level. The amount of information retained after every session is increased through her dynamic hands-on approach and peer-involvement.

Ben Longden, State Manager – NSW, Cookers Bulk Oil System

Renée's character, drive, passion and enthusiasm are infectious. Renée's knowledge and expertise have helped me develop as an individual for over five years. Through the Limitless Leaders program, I have seen a positive shift across two organisations. Most recently, Renée rolled out the Limitless Leaders program on Western Program Alliance, where we saw an increase in performance and collaboration among the team. I cannot thank Renée enough for the support and positive influence over the years.

Tiana Cologna, Project Operations Manager, Mott MacDonald

Renée is the quintessential leadership coaching professional who continually leads by example – captivating, authentic, inspirational and creative. She walks the talk – an energetic and adaptive life-long leadership student, continually growing and combining all of the essential leadership learnings to captivate, stimulate and educate. Renée's Skill Pills have been inspirational – they help you to chunk down all the essentials of leadership, collaboration and Growth Mindset, and she delivers them with such authenticity and creativity. Renée has a unique way of combining all of the leadership essentials and chunking them down into bite sized pieces for successful and effective 'digestible' implementation.

Tony Femia, State Manager VIC WA and SA, Retail Insurance Distribution

I was always in awe of Renée's ability to command a room and get people engaged – especially in a virtual environment. It was for this reason that I attended her Virtual Limitless Leaders Masterclass to enhance the leadership processes of my company. Renée's ability to deliver a range of effective and practical leadership strategies from a range of psychological principles is both extremely impressive and invaluable. As a doctoral student in psychology, I can appreciate the level of skill and knowledge that goes into producing real-life strategies from theory that actually work, which is a testament to her experience, intellect and level of skill. The course was very interactive and allowed us to gain strategies from Renée that were tailored to our specific needs. I have immediately began implementing these strategies within my work and found her approach to communication and rapport building especially valuable. A 'genuine expert' is the term that came to mind about Renée when I completed her virtual class.

Daniella Taranto, Managing Director, Recom Cleaning Pty Ltd

Renée is an amazing woman. Inspirational. She explains leadership strategies in a way that is easy to understand and provides suggestions of how to alter things leading to personal improvements. I particularly loved hearing about what 'lights me up'. Since our session, every day I have asked myself, 'Have I done something today that lights me up?' If I haven't, I try to do something, even if it is only little. My energy levels are up – thanks Renée. I am looking forward to our journey together and love that you're in my corner!

Natasha Groves, Account Manager, Opal – Converting Division

Renée facilitated a keynote on 'Change and Motivation from the Inside Out' at Telstra's National licensee roadshow in Melbourne. Her passion, subject matter expertise, and ability to deliver an engaging presentation were just what the audience needed. Renée's presentation set the tone for the remainder of the day and challenged all to think differently about how they personally lead through change. Thank you, Renée.

Jeff Yerbury, General Manager, Telstra Consumer and Small Business

Renée ran a series of virtual workshops for SPC at the onset of COVID when we were working from home. Renée was fantastic to work with, from custom designing the workshops to meeting our needs, through to the delivery, and participant documentation/post workshop support. The topics ranged from adopting a working from home mindset, collaboration, communication and personal branding (to name a few). We had excellent participant engagement and feedback.

Thanks Renée, my team and I really enjoyed working with you, and we highly value your expertise. We can't wait to work with you again.

Amanda McRoy, Senior Human Resources Leader

Renée has been my coach for over 12 months and is nothing short of incredible. Her advice is both technically brilliant and practical at the same time. All of her guidance is centred on motivations and values, which creates a win–win for both the individual and the workplace they ultimately thrive within. I also attended her Limitless Leadership program, which was a great refocus on the qualities a strong leader must exhibit. It is a great program for any leader trying to create a happy and productive workplace. I recommend Renée to any individual or organisation striving for success in a competitive environment.

Josy Shaw, Director of Marketing and Communications, Ovarian Cancer Australia Ltd

A big thank you to Renée Giarrusso for running the Openpay Mapping Motivation for Team Success workshop and the Limitless Leadership program. Renée's programs provided our team with a deep understanding of ourselves and each other in order to start working as a super team. They provided practical tools to help bridge some gaps, leverage each other's motivators, encourage collaboration, foster true partnerships and improve communication. Renée did a marvellous job of keeping a group of 50 people engaged for the entire day with her energy, enthusiasm and hands-on approach. More importantly, we noticed positive changes and results immediately! The Openpay team now feel better equipped to connect to each other and to our customers. We are now working more like a super team towards achieving our vision. I would highly recommend Renée and her support team to other businesses.

Marni Meydan, Director Operations, Meydan Group

Renée is a gifted management consultant with extensive experience in training, facilitation and executive coaching. She knows a variety of creative teaching methods to ensure you learn what you need to. Her calming and confident personality makes you feel comfortable and remain engaged during her sessions. Renée is excellent at encouraging trainees to have a go at difficult circumstances. She has an infectious great attitude. Renée is the best trainer I have ever had; there is no price worth her training sessions if you want to be a great manager and leader!

Joseph Kamara, Regional Director, Humanitarian and Emergency Affairs, East Africa, World Vision

Renée has been providing leadership guidance to GS1 Australia for the past five or so years. During that time, I have had the privilege of attending her Limitless Leadership workshops as well as regular coaching sessions to build on my own leadership and coaching skills. Renée's ability to adapt tools and models as frameworks to make the seemingly difficult seem simple has helped to restructure some of my thinking with an increased focus on leading strategically rather than working tactically. Her guidance has helped me to increase trust and openness in my team, which can only benefit the organisation as we strive to deliver our business objectives. Thank you Renée for being pragmatic, challenging and fun to work with!

Bonnie Ryan, Director – Freight, Logistics and Industrial Sectors, GS1 Australia

I was in the audience when Renée gave a keynote at a major industry conference. It was one of the best presentations I'd seen in years! She was dynamic, engaging, very persuasive and yet quite entertaining all at the same time. Renée knew how to connect with the audience powerfully and take the audience with her on the journey of leadership and change. Something that almost every organisation needs in these times.

Russell Wood, Senior Supply Chain and Systems Advisor,
Continuous Improvement Advisory